NEIL YOUNG

Neil Young

Reflections In Broken Glass

SYLVIE SIMMONS

2

CANONGATE

Originally published in hardback in the UK and simultaneously
in North America in 2001 by MOJO Books, an imprint of
Canongate Books, 14 High Street, Edinburgh EH1 1TE

This edition published in 2002

10 9 8 7 6 5 4 3 2 1

British Library Cataloguing-in-Publication Data
A catalogue record for this book is available on request
from the British Library

ISBN 1 84195 317 2

Typeset by Patty Rennie Production, Glenbervie
Printed and bound by Grafos, Spain

www.canongate.net

Contents

Acknowledgements

"THERE IS A SMALL AND SELECT GROUP OF ARTISTS so collectively unclassifiable that they can only be defined as 'The Awkward Squad'," Charles Shaar Murray once wrote, "each of them a one-person genre. However, the unchallenged Emir of Awkward is Neil Young." Provocative, changeable, ambiguous, capricious, his refusal to stay in one place physically, emotionally or musically is what has made him so uniquely fascinating. It also makes him hell to pin down in the pages of a book. By the time you read this, he'll no doubt have moved on in another new direction entirely, or done or said something that throws into question anything that's gone before. So I'll just shrug and do what I've assiduously avoided throughout the rest of the book and quote some of his lyrics back at him: "I've been wrong before and I'll be there again . . . I don't have any answers my friend, just this pile of old questions." This is the spot where I get to thank some of the people who helped me in my attempts to answer them.

For their opinions and support and access to their phone directories: Neil Adams, Sean Body, Denny Bruce, Jenny Bulley, David Dalton, Dave Di Martino, Bruce Gary, Harvey Kubernik. Thanks are also due to the Warner Brothers press office for the crate-loads of newspaper and magazine clippings, some of them old enough to carbon date, that they excavated from their archives, and to the fine human beings at MOJO, the best music magazine around.

The information and quotes in this book came from a number of sources, including interviews I personally conducted with Neil Young, Billy Talbot, Ralph Molina, Frank Sampedro, Joni Mitchell, David Crosby and Jim Jarmusch (for earlier projects) and with Ben Keith, Jerry Casale of Devo, Denny Bruce, Bruce Gary, Beck, Dennis Dragon, Domenic Priore and Johnny Cash (specifically for this one). A good deal of other fine material was culled from the interviews that have appeared in MOJO down the years by Nick Kent, John Einarson, David Fricke, Chris Heath, Barney Hoskyns, Jaan Uhelszki and Dave Di Martino (who also provided a helpful transcript of his interview with Crazy Horse). For the period up until the late '70s when Young kept a low profile from the press, I am highly indebted to interviews that appeared in Rolling Stone, especially those by Cameron Crowe (and his August '75 interview in particular). Among the other magazine interviews that proved highly useful were those by Ray Coleman in NME (Aug '73); Bud Scoppa in NME (June '75); Nick Kent in Vox (Nov '90); Allan Jones in Melody Maker (1990); Ben Thompson in The Independent On Sunday (Nov '92); Steve Sutherland in NME (July '95); Mark Cooper in Q (Sept '95);

David Fricke in Rolling Stone (April 2000).

There are a whole lot of books on Neil Young out there, and I think I can safely say I've read the whole darn lot of them (thanks to Sean Body, Emma Georgiou and Hugh Fielder for the loans). It probably wouldn't be politic to say what I think should be done with some of them, so instead I'll simply credit those that proved particularly enlightening: Neil Young: The Rolling Stone Files (1967–1980), Ghosts On The Road: Neil Young In Concert by Pete Long; Neil And Me by Scott Young; Crosby Stills Nash & Young and Neil Young: The Definitive Story Of His Musical Career by Johnny Rogan; There's Something Happening Here: The Story Of Buffalo Springfield For What It's Worth by John Einarson & Richie Furay; The Dark Stuff by Nick Kent; The Mansion On The Hill: Dylan, Young, Geffen, Springsteen And The Head-On Collision Of Rock And Commerce by Fred Goodman. The following were also useful: Long Time Gone: The Autobiography Of David Crosby by David Crosby & Carl Gottlieb; This Wheel's On Fire by Levon Helm with Stephen Davis; A Dreamer Of Pictures: Neil Young, The Man & His Music by David Downing; Don't Be Denied – Neil Young: The Canadian Years by John Einarson; Before The Goldrush, by Nicholas Jennings; Are You Ready For The Country by Peter Doggett.

The opening quotes of each chapter came from (Chapter One) The Dark Stuff; (Two) The Guardian, 1992; (Three) Neil And Me; (Four) MOJO, 1994; (Five) Rolling Stone, 1975; (Six) Q, 1988; (Seven) Q, 1995; (Eight) Melody Maker, 1989. Other uncredited quotes not from my own interviews were found in the following sources: (Chapter One) Rolling Stone; There's

Something Happening Here: The Story Of Buffalo Springfield For What It's Worth; The Dark Stuff; The Mansion On The Hill; A Dreamer Of Pictures: Neil Young, The Man & His Music; Mary Turner radio interview; Record Collector; NME; MOJO. (Chapter Two) Neil And Me; Pulse; Rolling Stone; Melody Maker; NME; The Dark Stuff; The Mansion On The Hill; Mary Turner; MOJO. (Chapter Three) Neil Young: The Rolling Stone Files; Neil Young And Broken Arrow: On A Journey Through The Past; Long Time Gone: The Autobiography Of David Crosby; Neil And Me; Mary Turner; Rolling Stone; VH1's Legends; Waiting For The Sun, Barney Hoskyns; Dave Di Martino; MOJO. (Chapter Four) Rolling Stone; Neil And Me; Ray Coleman/Melody Maker; Waiting For The Sun; NME; Melody Maker; Dave Di Martino; Neil Young: The Rolling Stone Files; Q; MOJO. (Chapter Five) Rolling Stone; A Dreamer Of Pictures; MOJO. (Chapter Six) A Dreamer Of Pictures; Neil And Me; Neil Young And Broken Arrow: On A Journey Through The Past; Rolling Stone; Melody Maker; The Mansion On The Hill; Guardian; Ghosts On The Road; Love To Burn by Paul Williams; NME; Vox; MOJO. (Chapter Seven) Q; Pulse; Times; Rolling Stone; Independent; NME; Rudiger Rapke internet interview; Neil And Me; Melody Maker; Total Guitar; Uncut; Mary Turner; MOJO. (Chapter Eight) Total Guitar; Rolling Stone; Mary Turner; NME; Observer; MOJO.

CALIFORNIA DREAMIN'

1 A Sort Of Sadness

There's a misbalance in my body ... I can feel it all the time.

THERE'S A HEARSE ROLLING ALONG THE freeway. Picked out by the oncoming headlights, the driver's face – pale, softly angular, framed by two slabs of backwoods sideburns and a Beatles cut – is set in a purposeful frown. The hearse's back windows are discreetly curtained, the front ones fogged from the cold night air and the smoke pluming out of the coffin compartment. Behind the curtains, someone's skinning up yet another number for the road. It's March 1966, and there's been something of an outbreak of young, long-haired dope-smokers driving old cars from the US to Canada to escape the Vietnam draft. The big, black '53 Pontiac, however, is heading the opposite way, Ontario to California. Hunched over the wheel, Neil Young, 20 years old and on "a mission from God", was doing four things that would prove to be archetypally Neil Youngesque: he was moving, crossing boundaries, taking a different direction from many of his contemporaries and, most important, he was in the driver's seat. There were several good reasons to head for Los Angeles. Apart from the obvious – it wasn't Canada, it was warm, and it was populated by girls with the looks that only widespread inbreeding among would-be stars and starlets could produce – it had by the mid-'60s supplanted New York as the pop music capital of America. This meant clubs to play and people to watch, notably people with music biz chequebooks. And in Los Angeles there was someone Young particularly wanted to play with: Stephen Stills. He'd met the Texan-born singer-guitar player in an Ontario folk club, and they'd talked about teaming up. This they might well have done when Young extinguished The

Squires – the group he'd formed aged 17 that Stills had been so impressed with – had it not been for a combination of immigration problems and a girlfriend convincing Young that he could be the next Bob Dylan.

Swapping his electric for a 12-string acoustic guitar, Young had hit the Ontario coffee-house circuit; it hit him back. The newspapers called him a "cliché"; he was getting nowhere fast. Broke, he signed on with The Mynah Birds, a folk-R&B-rock band who had a deal with Motown; however, their singer Rick James was hauled off by the military police as they were recording their debut and jailed for deserting a ship bound for duty in Vietnam. Young's attempt to track down Stills in New York while recording solo demos for a Canadian deal ended in failure on both fronts.

"I tried to keep my band going and then tried to work with several others but it just never worked out for me there . . . I just couldn't break into that scene," said Young, back once again in a cold Toronto winter, no money, just a bunch of band equipment with no band to play it and the radio booming out the big hit of the moment, The Mamas And The Papas' California Dreamin'.

Turning to Bruce Palmer, the bass player who'd recruited him for The Mynah Birds, he said, "Let's get out of here." Trading the equipment for a hearse and a bag of grass, they set off with four fuel-buying friends for the US border.

Talk to people who know or have worked with Young and the same words come up time and again: intense, stubborn, determined. Like that ant in the tropics that gets so stuck into its object of desire that if you tried to pull it off it would just tear clean down the middle, its ant-teeth still there in a permanent state of chew, the concept of backing off was not an option. As Elliot Roberts, his future manager, put it, "It was all life and death to Neil." He accomplished his "mission" only after a good deal of effort. En route he was hospitalised after collapsing in Albuquerque (Palmer interpreted Young's collapse as the first sign of his burgeoning epilepsy; Young insisted it was exhaustion, for which he only had himself to blame, having insisted on doing most of the driving on the basis that the others, especially the girls, didn't treat the old car right). And, when they finally made it to Hollywood, Stills was nowhere to be found.

For a week Young and Palmer trawled every club and bar in the city, sleeping in the hearse, taking tourists on rides around the stars' homes to make money for cigarettes and fuel. Their eventual meeting has become the stuff of rock legend: driving east down Sunset Boulevard to pick up the freeway to San Francisco to start searching again there, Young and Palmer were caught in a traffic snarl-up near the Chateau Marmont hotel; Stills was in a van coming the other way with Richie Furay, the singer-guitarist Young had met on his New York hunt for Stills. It was hard not to notice a hearse with Ontario licence plates. And in the car park of the nearby Liquor Locker market, a band was as near as dammit formed. "A great group," Young said. "Everybody was a fucking genius at what they did" – and just about everyone who saw them agreed. Young was in the perfect band at a time when being in a band was the place to be; as the innocence and youthful enthusiasm of the pop scene was on the cusp of morphing into the Us-And-Them team spirit of the counter-culture, bands were becoming the ultimate alternative community. But, Young being Young, it was not going to be long before he left and moved on.

"Try to isolate the one common denominator threading together Young's stout body of work and you have this image of characters constantly on the move," Nick Kent once observed. "Be they ancient Aztec warriors, motorcycle-riding waitress-divorcees, or, most often, guys who are a little paranoid and a little troubled, noble men-of-destiny types who smoke too much pot and analyse their own feelings too relentlessly, who are always looking out for a genuine soulmate but who are also aware they are way too self-obsessed to give enough of themselves to make any relationship truly work, so there is always this contradiction tugging at their souls like a sort of sadness."

The speed with which things came together for the band, even by the standards of the mid-'60s, was remarkable. Young and Palmer followed Stills and Furay back to their friend and manager Barry Friedman's house in old Hollywood and started playing. Friedman invited them to move in. After trying out a couple of drummers they settled on Dewey Martin – Young's choice; not only was he Canadian but he'd played with Roy Orbison, one of Young's favourite musicians – and the same day they found their fifth member they also found a name for the band on the plaque of a steamroller fixing up the road outside. Barely a week later, Buffalo Springfield were playing the National Orange Showgrounds in San Bernardino opening for The Byrds, followed in quick succession by a residency at the Whisky A GoGo, a supporting slot with the Stones at the Hollywood Bowl and a major label record deal.

Their endorsement by The Byrds didn't hurt; they were the cream of LA's folk-rock aristocracy, the band who had broken the club scene open for playing original material and still drawing crowds. The Springfield's kind of folk-rock was different – none of the jangle and Dylanisms, more electric country-psychedelia. "It had more of an older folk feel with country roots and acoustic alongside electric instruments," said Dickie Davis, sometime road manager and sound and lighting man at the Whisky – indeed, this was exactly what Stills had liked about Young's band The Squires: their electric surf-rock treatments of old American traditionals like Oh Susannah and Tom Dooley. Chris Hillman had been so impressed with the Springfield he discussed managing them with Roger McGuinn, before Sonny & Cher's managers Charlie Greene and Brian Stone took on the job. Hillman's opinion helped get them the house-band job at the small but prestigious two-year-old rock nightclub on Sunset, two doors down from the tiny London Fog where The Doors used to play and walking distance from the record companies and publishing offices that were springing up in the city.

The Whisky at that time was "the hottest place in the world to play", according to Domenic Priore, author of Riot On Sunset Strip: Rock'n'roll's Last Stand In Hollywood. "It was the nucleus of rock'n'roll at a very intense moment in history – all these people out there like Zappa and The Doors, but The Buffalo Springfield, everyone felt, were the wildest, the best, most rocking band of them all. Right away, within three weeks of playing, they were the hottest band on the Strip."

"The Whisky was as good as we ever were," said Richie Furay, "as close as we ever were, as unified, because we were working every day." For Bruce Gary, drummer with among others Albert Collins, Dr John and Jack Bruce, who saw several of the Springfield's Whisky shows, "They were one of the tightest bands I had ever seen. Their vocals were very impressive for that time in music. The interplay between the three guitars had to be experienced live to be fully appreciated."

The club had a different lay-out then from the one it has today (it's still in business, if considerably less splendid, hosting more local metal bands than legends). The stage was off to the left, underneath the overhang with the cages for the go-go girls. The tradition began when a female DJ up in her booth started dancing spontaneously one night and caused a large uptake in orders for long cool drinks from the male contingent in the crowd. "We knew them all," said Young, grinning. "We would look up there and say hi to them while we were playing. It was an inspiration! There were a lot of clubs to play and the Whisky was the best one, so when we got in there it was great. And these bands were coming in and out all the time." Though there wasn't much inter-band jamming – "at that time bands were a lot more independent" – there was a good deal of hanging out. Regulars included The Byrds, Love, The Mamas And The Papas and The Doors. "We all knew each other. I lived in the same piece of property with John Densmore, the drummer for The Doors."

"Incestuous, you ask?" said Bruce Gary. "This was the pre-AIDS, hippy-dippy-trippy, free-love, pot-smoking, acid-taking wonderland. There was a very close, communal sort of feeling amongst all of us that seemed to carry into wherever there were musical events." Said Priore, "Neil was a lot less reclusive back then than he was later. He used to hitchhike around LA with his friend, the woman who wrote the song Windy [Ruthann Friedman] and he hung with Jack Nitzsche, Ry Cooder and The Monkees; though everyone wrote them off as fakes, there was a big connection there and Neil played on the music for their movie Head." Stills had gone further, having been one of the 437 hopefuls who auditioned to join the band (rejected, reportedly, on the grounds of unphotogenic teeth). There was, of course, only so much "communal sort of feeling" a man like Neil Young could take before his innate separateness kicked in. Leaving the home he shared with the band, he rented a small wooden house high up in the hills above Sunset Boulevard.

"Neil found a log cabin – basically just one big

room – in Laurel Canyon, where all the cool people were," said Denny Bruce, drummer with The Mothers Of Invention, record producer and future Vanguard and Takoma Records boss. "To get to it you had to go up a whole bunch of stairs. It's really where he wrote a lot of the great songs. After they played the Whisky he would go back and write; he's always been a hard worker and dedicated to his craft." Certainly more dedicated than he was to the LA sex and drugs scene, which he tired of just as quickly. "It was sort of like a comet," was Young's recollection. "It was really intense then it just trickled off." Although "not", as Bruce recalled him, "the world's most sexual guy", there were nights when a girl would make the 15-minute drive from the club, climb the long flight of stairs, knock on the door, and clamber down again the next morning. The song Mr Soul was dedicated to the ladies of the Whisky A GoGo and the women of Hollywood. By the standards of, say, Led Zeppelin, the groupie scene was an innocent one, but it was there, and the Springfield – plastered over magazines like TeenSet and hailed as "the most good-looking and talented group to come along since The Beatles" – were definitely on the A-list.

The press had taken to calling the moody-looking guitar player "Neil The Indian" – something he didn't discourage, having spent his childhood devouring TV westerns and claiming a drop or two of Native American blood. The first thing Young bought with his Whisky earnings was a fringed jacket. And when he saw a Comanche war-shirt in a shop on Santa Monica Boulevard, he bought it and had two more made. ("The group was western, the name Buffalo Springfield came off a tractor, so it all fit.") "He was always looking for good imagery," said Bruce – all the more important now that the band had just signed with Atco, part of the Atlantic Records company.

"Young's is a pain-dominated, rather Old Testament sensibility," Bud Scoppa once wrote. Physical pain has certainly been a constant in his life – back operations, throat problems, two disabled children; when God went ringing doorbells in Ontario handing out the health breaks, Neil must have been out on one of his paper rounds. At the age of six he contracted polio; it left him with a weakness in the left side of his body and a slight limp that in later years, in tandem with his piercing glare, would give him an American gothic look. And soon after arriving in Los Angeles he had his first major epileptic seizure.

Young and Bruce Palmer were in a shopping mall; it was crowded, they were stoned. One minute Neil was standing up watching a salesperson demonstrate a vegetable-chopper and the next he was writhing on the floor. Doctors prescribed Dilantin and Valium. A second serious attack occurred when the Springfield were recording their debut album – while trying to feed the meter, Dickie Davis got into an altercation with a cop; Young came out to see what was happening and the officers of the LAPD took exception to his appearance. Finding that Young had outstanding parking tickets on the hearse – now requisitioned as a tour van (they could draw the curtains and smoke dope in the back, pull up to the gig, slide the coffin tray down to the pavement and painlessly unload the gear) – they took him in. In the few hours it took for the managers to stand his bail, he'd been beaten up, to the point where he was packed off to a neuropsychiatric hospital for tests. After that the attacks came more frequently.

"I don't know whether I just couldn't control it," said Young "or there were too many things happening to me. Whatever it was I'd just get this feeling inside of me and I'd just *go*."

"We got pretty adroit at handling Neil's seizures," said Davis. "He was taking medication daily but strobe lights would trigger them and he'd collapse on-stage. Richie stood nearest to him and would always grab his guitar before it hit the floor and we'd frantically yell at them to turn off the lights." Since the majority of attacks seemed to happen during the closing number (which for a long time was Mr Soul, itself written in hospital after he'd collapsed on-stage at an early show in Orange County), some people thought they were part of the show.

"We thought he used to stage [them] whenever there was a good-looking girl in the audience," said Dewey Martin. "He'd end up with his head in her lap, the girl wiping his brow." Added Denny Bruce, "That's why women loved the guy – they wanted to mother him. He didn't have to chase women, they came to protect him, brush his teeth, you know: 'You've got to take better care of yourself.'"

Young described his seizures to Rolling Stone's Cameron Crowe as "a very psychedelic experience ... You slip into some other world. Your body's flopping around and you're biting your tongue and batting your head on the ground, but your mind is off somewhere else. The only scary thing about it is . . . realising you're totally comfortable in this *void*. And that shocks you back into reality." Sometimes they were brought on by getting too high, other times by being in crowds. Often it was just pressure. "Neil's first attack," said Davis, "came within a month of meeting Stephen Stills. And as far as I know his last came shortly after he left the band for good."

2 The Dream Is Over

BANDS, THOUGH OFTEN VIEWED BY THEIR fans as microcosmic utopias, the ideal gang-cum-community, are every bit as hierarchical, competitive and dysfunctional as society at large, and generally a lot less democratic. The Springfield set-up was bound to cause difficulties: imagine The Who with three Pete Townshends and a Keith Moon who fancied himself as an Otis Redding. "Most of the time," said Dewey Martin, "we were able to get through songs without somebody getting angry and smashing their guitar or something – you know, baby stuff, prima donna stuff." Some of the time they didn't. Stephen Stills had voted himself leader –

perhaps through instinctive understanding that a band needs one; perhaps as a natural progression from having done so well at military school as a kid; then again, no-one has ever accused him of not having an ego. For a while it was tolerated, and the five individuals shuffled into their own power pyramid – Furay as lead singer, Stills as second lead, Young and Stills on lead guitar and so on – until it came to making records, when the issue of song-writing raised its head.

Their first single was to be Stills' Go And Say Goodbye backed with Young's Nowadays Clancy Can't Even Sing with Furay on lead vocal (Young had first played him the song when he met him in New York); by the time it came out, Young's song was on the A-side. And by the time it came to recording their eponymous debut album, the competition had intensified; arguments broke out over whose songs would go on. That Stills' songs outnumbered Young's by seven to five probably had more do with the first single's failure than with its quality, since Young was already proving himself the more interesting writer with ambitious material like Flying On The Ground Is Wrong. Stills, however, had come up with their first hit record: For What It's Worth, inspired by the 1966 riots on Sunset Strip. The LAPD, concerned at the youth mecca the street had become, and in cahoots with a group of developers who wanted to close the sprawl of rock clubs and build a business district, decided to crack down. The club-goers, students mostly, led a protest; 300 were arrested. The heavy-handedness of the "Sunset Pigs", combined with a growing mid-'60s anti-authoritarianism as young people saw their peers coming home from Vietnam in body-bags, turned the incident into a Statement and the song into an Anthem.

Young was nervous in the recording studio, mostly about his vocals. As Furay recalled, his main role in the band at first had been guitar player and writer: "Steve was pretty much set on singing his own songs, although as The Beatles did we would sing unison on quite a few songs and then break into harmonies. I sang most of Neil's songs early on. I felt I could sing Neil's songs better than Neil could." Singing had long been an insecurity. The Squires started out as an instrumental band; when Young first added vocals on-stage in January '64, someone shouted, "Stick to instrumentals!" The recording engineer who worked on The Squires' single had told him, "You're a good guitar player, kid, but you'll never make it as a singer." His high, tense, tremulous voice with its haunting, plaintive undertow – variously described as "evoking Skip James, one of the great Delta Bluesmen" (Dave Marsh, MOJO) and "pre-adolescent whining" (Rolling Stone) – was always going to polarise people, as any Neil Young fan with unconverted friends can attest. Intimate but retaining a sense of distance and dislocation, his voice was seen by fellow-Canadian Joni Mitchell as having "a lot of Prairie" in it. Whatever way you looked at it, it was intense.

But what ultimately disappointed Young about the finished album was the band's sound. It just didn't sound real. And the reason, as Young saw it, was because it wasn't the live sound they had on-stage. "When we got into the studio the groove just wasn't the same and we couldn't figure out why," he said. "This was the major frustration – it fucked me up so much. We had a great rhythm section and a really good beat live, but we just didn't get it on record." The few recordings he had made before had been live ones. "When I got down to LA with The Buffalo

Springfield it was just about the time multi-track recording was starting to come in. It took a while for me to realise that I liked to sing and play all at once." His bandmates, too, were unhappy with the album, to the point of petitioning their managers to get the record company to let them scrap it and start again. But Greene and Stone, with their Sonny & Cher background, were more old-school music biz people from a singles culture, and talked them out of running up more expense. Released in January '67, *Buffalo Springfield* piqued the interest of rock writers but failed to make much impact on the charts.

Though the lack of instant success didn't help matters, the cracks were already showing in the band. For some time there had been mutterings about getting rid of Dewey Martin (at one time Skip Spence had been mooted as a replacement, after leaving Jefferson Airplane and before joining Moby Grape). In the end, Bruce Palmer was first to go – less than voluntarily, having been jailed and deported to Canada in April '67 following a marijuana bust – replaced, depending on what day you're talking about, by Jim Fielder, Bob West, Dick Davis or Young's old

Squires sidekick Ken Koblun. Palmer's departure was swiftly followed by Neil Young's. Sessions for a second album, to be called *Stampede*, were even more turbulent than those for the first, with squabbles over songs, arrangements and leadership coming to a head in an argument over scheduled appearances at the Monterey Pop Festival and on the popular, mainstream TV programme The Tonight Show With Johnny Carson.

"I couldn't handle it," Young explained in a 1979 radio interview. "I don't know why, but something inside of me felt like I wasn't quite on track. I don't know, I had a really negative attitude about all of those things, about the pop festivals. I wasn't really into it . . . I didn't know if the people could hear us." As for the Tonight show, "I thought it was belittling what The Buffalo Springfield was doing," he told MOJO. "We'd have been just a fucking curiosity to them." If these two stances appear mutually contradictory – to refuse to play a free hippie music festival, while also resisting selling out to commercial television, siding with 'Us' instead of 'Them' – they were totally in keeping with the mess of contradictions that always informed Young's outlook. Apart from the one simple fact that Young had never been, nor ever would be, an 'Us' (witness a later interview with a young American activist who tried to enlist his support for a campaign to legalise pot; when talk turned to revolution, Young said if it came they'd find him "in Big Sur with my guns [and] material gains"), what his outlook demonstrated most of all was a stubborn integrity and cynicism and, when it came to the whole hippie deal, a well-developed bullshit detector. (As it happened he was right to be cynical about Monterey; fabulous show though it was, it was also one of the first nails in the coffin of rock's peace-love-freedom consciousness and marked the onset of music biz decadence and greed.)

Doug Hastings of The Daily Flash was recruited to replace Young on record while David Crosby of The Byrds stood in at Monterey. Though he'd initially told Chris Hillman, "They suck; I don't like them", by the time of his autobiography, Long Time Gone, Crosby had revised his opinion. "The first time I heard Stephen and Neil play guitar together I heard a conversation, not a competition: the best kind of lead guitar I'd ever heard outside of Jimi Hendrix." Young agreed. If the competitiveness had driven him out, the musical dialogue brought him back, and he persuaded the managers to get him in the band again. A second attempt was made at recording an album, this time with Atlantic chief Ahmet Ertegun producing, but once again the mood was fractious – too much for Koblun who quit and went back to Canada. Palmer's return – he'd snuck across the border – raised Young's spirits for a while, but not for long; the hapless bassist was soon arrested and deported a second time. To add to the tension, the band had just fired their managers (substituting Nick Grillo, who looked after The Beach Boys).

Meanwhile, the studio was increasingly being filled with the kinds of hangers-on that bands with a growing reputation attract – drug-dealers, groupies, people trying to sell them stuff or just be part of the gang. Though the other Springfields didn't appear to object too much, they made Young nervous. He had never liked being around crowds of people, unless on a stage and out of their way; and as the incident in the shopping mall had shown, neither they nor the drugs they brought with them were particularly good for his health. This feeling of separateness translated into what was going on in the studio: like the band's new single, Bluebird backed with Mr Soul (a situation Young was less than happy with), Stills was on one side and Young on the other, and they were rarely in the studio at the same time. But the music they were coming up with was superb. "We were just really discovering a lot of new things and experimenting."

Buffalo Springfield Again, as their second album was renamed, was hailed as a country-psychedelic-rock classic. But by the time it appeared on the cusp of '67/'68, the band that rock encyclopaedist Lillian Roxon said "had all the markings of the group of the '6os" was on the verge of falling apart.

Young had been working on – and occasionally recording – some of his songs on the second album with his new friend Jack Nitzsche – "one of the modern-day masters; his creations are on a par with Mozart". Young had first met Nitzsche – who, among other things, had co-authored Needles And Pins, had his own instrumental hit The Lonely Surfer and was eccentric genius Phil Spector's equally idiosyncratic arranger – at his manager's office;

Greene and Stone had installed a pool table and encouraged musicians to hang out. "But they never got to know each other musically," said Denny Bruce, "because Neil was locked up with all these people and Jack was working with the Stones. Then I was at Neil's log cabin one night and he started playing a song and said, 'This is something I'd like to hear The Everly Brothers do.' And I said, Hey, Jack Nitzsche is going to be working with them. This was before you could just make a cassette of your song – there were no cassette machines! – so I spoke to Jack and he said, 'Yeah, I really like his writing, Nowadays Clancy Can't Even Sing', and we got together and I said, Neil, play that Everly Brothers thing, Expecting To Fly. After one verse Jack said, 'Fuck The Everly Brothers, *you're* doing this song', and they went into the studio without the Springfield and used studio guys. And that really set Neil apart. People started calling from England – Graham Nash said it was the best record he'd ever heard. So that's when it started, 'Well, maybe we should move to England.' Jack was connected with the Stones and The Walker Brothers so it made a lot of sense."

Since Nitzsche had just separated from his wife

and Denny Bruce was staying with him, the three decided to take a place together while making arrangements for Young's escape from the Springfield. "We lived in this crazy place called the bubble house, a clear plastic house on the hillside, awaiting the move to England," said Bruce. "We'd got our passports, we were ready. Then they started playing Mr Soul on the radio and the DJ said, 'That was when Neil was with them, baby.' With that Neil went back into the Springfield and Jack and I moved out of the bubble house. I still think Neil's best records were the ones Jack worked on. When you listen to Expecting To Fly, the chord changes, the tempo changes, were really different from what most other bands were doing and the lyrics, to read them, are poetry."

They'd sit around the house together, listening to music. "He loved talking about pop music with me," said Bruce, "because I had a great record collection – he really liked Jeff Beck and Hendrix; you can tell what he got into on the electric guitar – and he'd listen to sounds and try to figure out how to do it. The Wind Cries Mary blew his mind because the chords, I guess, are kind of like a country song. There's a line in there, something like 'he's looking for a queen', and Neil would say, '*I* would have said this.' He was always evaluating songs." Talking about his own lyrics, Young revealed to Bruce that it wasn't, as is generally thought, acid (which by that time had supplanted pot as LA's drug of choice) that inspired songs like Flying On The Ground Is Wrong.

"He wasn't on drugs then, except his medication to prevent epileptic seizures – he would smoke pot once in a while and that's it. He told me he had this feeling that he was falling in slow motion, where he had to calm down; that's what all those early songs like Burned, The Old Laughing Lady, Falling Down and Helpless are about."

In the end Young's epilepsy was as big a factor as ego in his decision to leave the Springfield for good; the pressure of being in the band was starting to get too much. "Neil got very dizzy, said he got headaches," said Greene. "And Stephen said, 'Go fuck yourself.'" Young's then girlfriend, folk singer Robin Lane, remembered him not feeling up to making a band rehearsal one night and Stills bursting into the cabin yelling, "You're ruining my career!", grabbing her guitar to smash on his bandmate's head.

A tour had been set up with The Beach Boys and The Strawberry Alarm Clock in the South – not the calmest place to play, what with the recent murder of Martin Luther King. But the band, near bankrupt, needed the cash, so in April '68 they set off on what would be The Buffalo Springfield's final tour. "The uptightness that was happening at the time was a major bummer," recalled Beach Boys percussionist Dennis Dragon. "The tour schedule was such that it was causing major problems with everybody – we were doing two and three shows a day, in different areas – and the pressure was becoming so much that Neil was having seizures regularly. I was witnessing all this stuff – one of them happened on-stage and it was not a pretty sight. It was out of control, and his health was going crazy, and I am about 100 per cent sure that that's what broke them up." Though The Beach Boys had discovered Transcendental Meditation since the last time the Springfield toured with them, and insisted their support band recite mantras, it would take a lot more than that to restore peace and love to the imploding band. A third album was patched together by Richie Furay and Jim Messina, the band's engineer-turned-bass player, *Last*

Time Around. But by its August '68 release the band had long broken up.

"I knew they weren't going to last," said Denny Bruce. "It's like being on a sports team where one guy wants the ball more than the others and as the coach always says, 'It's too bad we don't have more balls, there's only one ball and only one guy can shoot it.' In the Springfield there were just too many microphones, too many guitars, and Neil needed his own space. I went to their last ever concert with Neil in a limo along with Jack Nitzsche. Neil really enjoyed himself. On the way back Jimmy Messina asked for a ride and he cried the whole ride home. He hated to see the thing end. Neil felt sorry for Jimmy, but for him it was almost a celebration. He was relieved."

"We thought we were going to be together for about 15 years," said Young, pictured looking away from his colleagues on the sleeve of *Last Time Around*, "because I knew how good it was." It lasted a little over two. All of their albums, he said, had been "failures".

WILL THE LAST TO LEAVE THE
'60s TURN OFF THE LIGHT

3 Back In The Saddle

There's a saying that once you've looked the Devil in the eye, there'll always be more Devil in you than there was before.

DURING BUFFALO SPRINGFIELD'S BRIEF IF influential existence, the LA scene had changed considerably. By the end of '67 many of the clubs were closing and the bands scrambling around for new places to play. "LA started borrowing the San Francisco small ballroom thing," said Domenic Priore, "and the extended boogie playing that went on in these places came with it too – Young and Stills started getting into that kind of playing, whereas at the Whisky their songs were still short. One scene closed and turned into another." The "happy young teenage scene" on the Sunset Strip had dislocated, became something tenser and darker, its "innocent craziness" giving way to just plain craziness. "Post-Easy Rider, there was this feeling among a lot of people on the scene of wanting to get out of the city, of wanting to be ranchers and farmers or just move on. Which is when Neil Young got out. He had his health problems to deal with and he couldn't be around all this pressure."

"It wasn't me scheming on a solo career," Young would later explain. "It wasn't anything but my nerves. Everything started to go too fucking fast ... I needed more space." He got the space courtesy of the solo career, spending his record company advance on a house out of town in rustic Topanga Canyon. It gave him, he said, "something solid" – an unusual craving for a rock musician in his early years, though perhaps not for one who had discovered that "personal stability" controlled his epilepsy better, and with less unpleasant side-effects, than drugs.

Twenty miles west of Hollywood, Topanga was

greener and woodier than Laurel Canyon, the previous rock star sanctuary of choice. The hills were higher and more treacherous so the cops kept their distance, and its houses were much further apart. "You could be as cowboy as you wanted," said Denny Bruce; some of its residents used horses to get about.

"The community was rich with artists and musicians," said Bruce Gary, who moved there in '67 and found Spirit, Linda Ronstadt, Taj Mahal, John Densmore, Canned Heat and Crazy Horse among his neighbours. "The first settlers of musical note were Woody Guthrie and Ramblin' Jack Elliott – Woody bought a house on a large patch of land there in the '50s and Jack lived in a house on the same land. When they moved out he sold the land to actor Will Geer, who was kind of the spiritual godfather of Topanga and supervised local events. There was a natural amphitheatre on his land. On any given day it was a place to hear and participate in some jamming."

So was the Topanga Corral, the small club with the spacious room and good sound-system where Gary played with Albert Collins and in Buckwheat, a band that featured the Springfield's Bruce Palmer on bass. "All the local musicians played there. I remember walking in one night to find Janis Joplin playing pool – she sang a few blues songs with the band playing that night. Neil and Crazy Horse played there often. Canned Heat must have played there 500 times. The other place to hang out in the evenings was the Moonfire Inn – a small coffee house near the centre of the canyon that hung on a cliff over the creek. Taj Mahal was frequently there playing in the corner by the fireplace. This is where Neil met his first wife Susan, who worked there – a very pretty and soft-spoken blonde-haired girl." Marrying Susan Acevado in December '68 made Young's solidity and stability complete: an attractive and (presumably, since she ran a restaurant) domesticated wife with a seven-year-old daughter; cats, dogs and a goat in the yard; a two-storey, redwood-panelled house on stilts with a view of the entire canyon – if Young had remotely resembled a hippie this would have been the hippie dream.

The final part of the solidity/stability equation was getting someone he trusted to handle the business pressures. Elliot Roberts had come up through the William Morris Agency in New York – the music biz equivalent of the Marines – working alongside the infamously hard-headed David Geffen before quitting to manage Joni Mitchell. When Mitchell was in Los Angeles recording her debut album with then boyfriend David Crosby producing, the Springfield were working in the studio next door. Joni and Neil had first met on the coffee-house scene in Winnipeg. He played her a song written in a motel room on his nineteenth birthday, Sugar Mountain, to which she wrote The Circle Game in response. She felt a kindred spirit with him. Both of them had caught polio in the same Canadian epidemic; both of them were "pensive" and wrote songs "from the inner landscape" because the outside world "looked fearful". They were very difficult times," said Mitchell. "You had the war on TV and police with barbed-wire bumpers coming up against Yippie candlelight parades. America was swaying from the death of Kennedy – Daddy was dead, what will happen to us? What will happen to the world?" Neil told her his dream was to own a chicken farm.

At the same time Mitchell found him to be one of the funniest people she had ever known, the reason she gave Roberts for meeting him. Before you make any rash judgements about Canadians, several others had said the same thing of the man his former room-mate Denny Bruce described in somewhat less surprising terms as "a sad Scorpio who liked to wear black clothing and who was only into music". As his friend and producer David Briggs told Young's father Scott, "He was such a great writer of moody ballads that everyone's perception of him as a person was totally different from what the guy is really like. You analyse his songs and everybody thinks here's this melancholy guy, this tortured, inner-looking person. But from the first minute I knew him I saw him as a prankster and a joker, a happy-go-lucky guy who loved to hang out and have fun." And David Crosby found him "one of the funniest human beings alive. He's a hysterically funny person if he knows you and he likes you. He's very reserved and weird if you don't know him." Roberts and Young quickly hit it off. A few weeks later, Young showed up at his door in Laurel Canyon, told him he was leaving the Springfield and asked Roberts to manage him. He has done so ever since.

In between fixing up his new house, Young was

making his debut solo album, assisted by Jack Nitzsche, who had helped secure his solo deal – his instrumental The Lonely Surfer had been one of Reprise's first pop hits, so he had good access to label chief Mo Ostin, to whom he talked up his friend. Also on board were Ry Cooder and David Briggs. Briggs had moved to Topanga from Wyoming a few years earlier and met Young when the singer was hitchhiking around the Canyon looking for a place to buy; the producer picked him up in his old army van and invited him to stay on his couch. Although Briggs would later become identified with Young's rawest, most live-sounding albums – "some of my best records," as Young said, "my favourites anyway" – *Neil Young*, released in the US at the end of '68 and in Britain as late as September '69, was not one of them. Young, Briggs said, was "a really immediate guy" and *Neil Young* was nowhere near immediate enough. Far too long had been spent on the grandiose arrangements and turgid production that often swamped the vocal – partly deliberate, since he continued to be insecure about his singing ("I was paranoid about my voice, so on my first LP I buried my voice intentionally"), and partly the unfortunate effect of a new, untested studio device his record company had generously given him which was supposed to make everything sound wonderful but instead "screwed everything up".

Certainly a sparer, more intimate sound would have suited much of the material's compelling mix of innocence and cynicism, confusion and anger, paranoia and melancholia. Songs like the nine-minute Dylanesque epic Last Trip To Tulsa elaborated on the tense paranoia of Nowadays Clancy Can't Even Sing, the early song he gave to the Springfield, and echoed the sour view of stardom he had even back when he was one fifth – and not the most visible fifth – of a band. I've Been Waiting For You, If I Could Have Her Tonight and I've Loved Her So Long approached love and relationships as either unattainable or destined to fail (quite what his new wife made of this is open to question), painting a picture not of a man in a pretty comfortable domestic set-up in a beautiful house on a hill but a tortured, questing, solitary romantic. With the song The Loner, it was an image that was established in many people's minds for good – despite the fact that he didn't plan to stay alone for long.

*

Back when The Buffalo Springfield were recording their debut, Young's then girlfriend Robin Lane had introduced him to a friend of hers, Danny Whitten of The Rockets. The six-piece band – Whitten, Leon and George Whitsell, Bobby Notkoff, Billy Talbot and Ralph Molina – had grown out of the guitar player's earlier a cappella outfit with Talbot and Molina, Danny And The Memories. "They were definitely the first garage band I ever knew," said Lane. "They smoked pot and sold it and jammed." Since their place was nearby in Laurel Canyon, it was easy for Young to jam with them. He loved the band's loose, simple sound, and their easy-going attitude was in stark contrast to the Springfield's warring egos: "There wasn't any of the pressure or the hyperness or posing that took part in the other bands." Over time a close friendship had grown between Young and Whitten – it was Danny who helped him conquer his insecurities about his voice and encouraged him to sing – but, thanks to his Springfield commitments, some time had passed without them seeing each other when Young got a call from Molina telling him that they were playing the Whisky and that he should come along and sit in. Which he did. By that time the Springfield had broken up. The Rockets were soon to break up as well. Young had written some new songs that he wanted to perform with a band – specifically The Rockets' bassist, drummer and guitar player. "It just," he said, "felt *right*." Naming them Crazy Horse, Neil The Indian followed his solo debut with *Everybody Knows This Is Nowhere*, which gave equal billing to his new band. They had been together just three weeks when they recorded one of the finest albums of Young's – or anyone's – career.

Three of its key songs, significantly perhaps, had been written in a state of bad health: he was in bed with a 103-degree fever when he called Whitten, Talbot and Molina to come over and play Cinnamon Girl, Cowgirl In The Sand and Down By The River, dark, passionate songs full of tension and dread about violence, lust and obsession. The last of the three, said Young, was "a desperation cry" from someone who "let the dark side come through a little too bright" – again not exactly what you might expect from a newly-married man. Apart from Round & Round, which featured his ex-girlfriend Robin on backing vocals, this was a decidedly male record. The exhilarating instrumental work-outs were only possible through the Horse's male-bonding support; they gave him not only confidence, but a solid, muscular rhythm that served as a springboard for the raw, bleeding hunks of sound he ripped out of his guitar. "Crazy Horse is a very soulful feeling for me," he said. "They give me a support that no-one else can give me, they afford me the possibilities of doing more with my guitar and my voice and feeling than anybody else."

"When we get together and play it's just *real*," Molina explained. "I'm a feeling type of drummer and Neil is a feeling type of guitar player and music is a feeling thing – his emotion draws ours and ours draws his, that's the way it works. You can go to school and learn charts and everything but I don't think those guys are real happy." And it's certainly not what Young was after. The first time he heard The Rockets – back when some people were referring to the Springfield as the American Beatles – they had struck him as an "American Rolling Stones". "I know my musician friends, a lot of people, think we play simple and there is no finesse and everything, but we're not trying to impress anybody, we just want to play with the feeling," Young said. "It's like a trance we get into." The first time he'd ever found himself getting into that trance, possessed by his guitar playing, was during a set with The Squires when he was 19 years old; something switched in him and he just started "transcending", he said. "Things just got on to another plane. Afterwards people would say, 'What the hell was that?' That's when I started to realise I had the capacity to lose my mind playing music," and the realisation fascinated him.

There was a disconnectedness and brutal intensity to his guitar playing with Crazy Horse that he would rarely if ever find elsewhere, as he dug deep inside himself and dragged his demons to the surface. Among them were the illnesses that had plagued him. The impression he sometimes gave of his right and left hands having different agendas at the same time reflected the continuing weakness from the childhood polio that slowed down one side of his body; the finger-jammed-in-a-live-wire one-note solos and the musical trances summoned up his epileptic seizures. At times when he played guitar he would almost pass out, unaware that in his search for "notes that aren't there" he had forgotten to breathe. His guitar style, instantly identifiable, was "just a big, distorted mess", he said, but "occasionally other things come out of it – a lot of clear things. I like that."

Young had no intention of making the same mistake recording his new band that he had with The Buffalo Springfield: *Everybody Knows This Is Nowhere* would be made as naturally and spontaneously as possible. Running Dry featured his first recorded 'live' vocal; singing and instrumental jams were recorded simultaneously on several tracks. Producer David Briggs was in his element. "His communication with Neil was very special," said Briggs's friend Bruce Gary, who hung out at some of the sessions. "He had an innate sense of getting the right combination of sounds and atmosphere." The mood in the studio was loose and light-hearted, fuelled by cheap-but-potent Red Mountain Wine; the album they came out with was a masterpiece.

Everybody Knows This Is Nowhere was Young's breakthrough. It climbed into the US Top 30 and was heading for gold when Young made the surprise announcement that he was leaving Crazy Horse for Crosby, Stills & Nash.

4 Bad Trip

WHEN 33-YEAR-OLD CHARLES MANSON WAS
released from the latest of a long list of jail sentences in
1967, he headed straight for freak mecca San Francisco.
The radio that year, like a counter-culture ad agency, had
played nothing but Scott McKenzie's and The Flowerpot
Men's paeans to the place, and Haight-Ashbury was ripe
with drifters, drop-outs and doped-up innocents for the
picking. Manson wouldn't have been out of place, even
with his prison haircut, among the neighbourhood's
gurus, weirdos and revolutionaries. He wrote songs and
played guitar (learned in jail from a survivor of the
infamous '30s Ma Baker gang), had a gift for mystical-

metaphysical ramblings, talked about setting up a musical commune in the California desert – The Family Jams – and had acquired a big black bus in which to take his followers there. Not a lot different on the surface from fellow former jailbird and bus-owner Ken Kesey's Merry Pranksters, other than their leader's prison records (Manson's included theft, burglary, pimping and rape; Kesey's possession of marijuana), the diversity of their followers (Manson's were mostly lost hippie girls and some weak-willed guys) and their particular revolutionary subgenre (Manson's paranoia centred on an apocalyptic race war).

Getting loaded and listening closely to albums to decode and discuss their secret meanings was a normal late '6os activity; at the end of '68, studying The Beatles' *White Album* at Spahn Ranch, the desert hideaway where his Family were waiting out the coming Armageddon, he found confirmation and full details of his beliefs in its lyrics. It would all come down, The Beatles assured him, in the summer of '69 in Los Angeles. So Manson and the Family set off for Topanga Canyon.

"I remember seeing Manson hanging out at the

Topanga centre market," said Bruce Gary. The girls used to raid the rubbish bins outside for discarded food with expired sell-by dates; after a while the store, in true '60s community spirit, would put it on one side for them. If the Canyon's seclusion and topography were ideal for Manson, its tolerant, outlaw population of hippies, freaks, bikers and musicians was perfection. Particularly the musicians and rock stars. Charlie had long hair, wild eyes and a guitar; he thought he was God and the Devil rolled into one. He fitted in perfectly. Neil Young's redwood house high up in the Canyon's Fernwood Pacific section was just one of the musicians' pads where Charlie hung out with his guitar and his girls. "The last thing Charlie wanted was a music career, but everybody wanted to have him at their party. Dennis Wilson wanted to live with us . . . Dennis loved Charlie," wrote Family member Sandra Good. "But we got along with everybody, actually."

Dennis Wilson had met Manson through the two Family girls he'd picked up hitchhiking and taken back to his house for sex; Young had met Manson through Wilson, whom he'd befriended on the first Springfield-Beach Boys tour; and Neil's wife Susan knew the girls because they would come and clean up at her restaurant in exchange for food – in the unreconstructed '60s they must have seemed just like any other nice, obliging chicks providing one more willing service for their man.

Manson was "great", Young recalled. "He was unreal. He was really, really good. Scary. Put him with a band that was as free as he was, no-one was ever going to catch up with Charlie Manson because he'd make up the songs as he went along." Linda Kasabian and Patricia Krenwinkle sat either side of Young on his couch while they listened to Manson play his guitar and sing his songs. Two intense, lank-haired Scorpios, masters of the mad stare, sitting in the same room high above a canyon with devoted women hanging on their every word and note; it makes quite a picture. Young admitted he found Manson fascinating. Any strangeness he put down to the fact that the man had spent over half his life in prison and was unfamiliar with the ways of the outside world – and anyhow, as his manager Elliot Roberts once pointed out, Young had a "weakness" for "difficult people".

Young and Manson shared not only a jaundiced and separatist outlook (the words of one Manson song –

"With your cardboard houses and your tin can cars/You sit and wonder, you wonder where you are" would have been right at home on Young's 1974 album, *On The Beach*) they had a similar taste in music. Manson, who was heavily into Hank Williams and Lefty Frizzell, favoured a spontaneous, unedited musical approach that put even Young's to shame. "He never sang the same song twice," said Young. "He made the songs up as he went along. Each song was a new one, every time he sang." The notes that Family member Sandra Good wrote on their *Family Jams* album could have as easily applied to Young: "The words would come spontaneously . . . Manson's music moves you because it's authentic, it's whatever's coming through him at that time, that point in now." Young was so taken with it that he spoke to his record company's chief, Mo Ostin, about making Charlie his labelmate. "I told him that I'd met this guy who I thought was a very unique individual. Very special but very wild." He did warn him too that "Charlie was a little . . . intense." Too intense, in the end, even for Young. A wall went up way before Manson had worked out that if The Beatles' prophecies were going to come true, someone would have to start the summer of '69 murder spree that was meant to ignite his promised race war. He dispatched his followers to Beverly Hills where they butchered film director Roman Polanski's wife, Sharon Tate, and the pregnant actress's four guests, scrawling messages on the wall in the victims' blood. Two days later they struck again at the Los Feliz mansion of a wealthy businessman.

"When you need a monster one will appear," wrote David Dalton, who interviewed Manson at the time of the murders. "He is a demon of the *Zeitgeist*. Appearing with almost supernatural precision in the last months of the '60s, he seemed to call into question everything about the counter-culture. His malign arrival synchronised so perfectly with America's nervous breakdown that it is hard not to bestow occult meanings on him." Manson was either the Anti-hippie, or the Ultimate-hippie, hippie-dom's home-grown Final Solution, depending on how you looked at it. As the case turned into a sensational media circus that distracted viewers from the sight of defeated young US soldiers coming home dead or damaged from Vietnam, Manson's drug-crazed, drop-out "monstrous love and terror cult" was held responsible not only for a "massacre" of Hollywood's richest and finest but for all the ills and confusions of the decade – the kind of summer bummer that even the three-day peace-and-love Woodstock Festival couldn't neutralise.

With perfect timing, exactly one week after the slayings Young and his new sidekicks Crosby, Stills and Nash were making their name as the supreme '60s peace-and-love band at Woodstock, where over a half a million stardusted, golden children of God were enjoying the last innocent taste of the fruits of the hippie Garden of Eden before the skies blackened and the Monster was unleashed. Even after Manson's arrest, a paranoia hung over America's Beautiful People, especially in California. A dark incubus had gate-crashed the hippie dream and was sucking the life out of it, nourished by the increasing ugliness, isolationism, egos and greed of LA's fragmenting rock scene. By the last big rock show of the decade – the December 1969 free festival at Altamont Speedway in Northern California headlined by The Rolling Stones – there wasn't a single drop left.

CSN&Y, with perfect congruity, having played at Woodstock, the '60s major light festival, played at its dark finale too. "It was the hippie nightmare," said Young. "That was a ridiculously, absurdly, psychedelically bad day" – a day of drug overdoses, tension and violence that culminated in the murder of a black teenage fan by the Hell's Angels who'd been brought in to handle security. Employing them had been The Grateful Dead's idea; what seems absurd now wouldn't have seemed so out of place to a community for whom the alternative would have been the less than counter-culture-friendly cops and who'd seen bikers sanctioned by the film Easy Rider as one of 'Us'.

If the Manson murders had put the '60s on trial, Altamont found it guilty. The caretaker at 10,050 Cielo Drive hadn't heard Sharon Tate's screams as they gutted her because he was playing, full volume, a Doors record; while the Hell's Angels were setting on the Altamont crowd, The Grateful Dead were cowering in their trailer; CSN&Y, who would have left if Crosby the hippie hadn't talked them into playing, did a quick, desultory set then got the hell out and played a gig back in LA.

On a trawl through the endless websites devoted to Charles Manson over 30 years after the murders, I came across a long interview in which he talked about his former musician friends. He said he'd liked Dennis Wilson although The Beach Boys had cheated him, never coming through with the Rolls-Royce they'd offered him in exchange for songs he gave them. The only one who'd given him something was Neil Young, he said, who gave him a motorcycle. The perfect vehicle, all things considered, on which to ride out the hippie apocalypse.

MAID SERVICE

5 A Very Very Very Fine House

Neil likes to play in groups, but basically he's a solo artist. I don't think he'll ever stay with any group for long.

Danny Whitten

CROSBY, STILLS & NASH AND *EVERYBODY KNOWS This Is Nowhere*, the two hit albums that soundtracked the summer of '69, couldn't have been much more different. One acoustic, optimistic and harmonious, the other electric, tormented and brutal, they might have stood for the polarised state of the counter-culture as the '60s ended. It couldn't have occurred to Crazy Horse that within weeks of the release and of taking them from The Rockets he would leave them to join Crosby, Stills & Nash. If *Everybody Knows* had been a flop, or anything less than brilliant, or if Stephen Stills hadn't already proven injurious to Young's health, it might have been easier to understand. The various reasons Young gave could basically be boiled down to two: a wish to protect himself from the spotlight while still continuing to make music ("It's a lot easier being part of a bigger group because the centre of attention isn't so much on you"); and to continue to make that music with whomever he damn well liked. His new passion – writing and making films, which he screened at the local Topanga community hall – had whetted his appetite for casting specific people in different roles, and though he loved Crazy Horse's simplicity he also had another side to him that was "technically too far advanced" for them, he said, "so the other band plays that".

Crosby, Stills & Nash's reasons for wanting Young, however, came down to just one: in order to turn the three-man vocal group into a successful touring band they needed extra instrumentation, specifically guitar and keyboards. They'd approached, and been turned down by, Stevie Winwood and John Sebastian before Ahmet Ertegun, the head of their label, Atlantic Records, suggested talking to Stills's old sparring partner. Crosby, the group's house hippie, was the most enthusiastic; Nash, afraid of damaging a good thing, was initially the least. Stills thought it might work as long as it was made quite clear to Young that he was only being hired as a sideman. Young quickly made it clearer that if they wanted him, it would have to be on his terms: "You have to change the name because if I'm coming, for me to give my whole soul and spirit to this, it has to be four ways – payment, respect, name on the marquee." And so CS&N became the quite different animal CSN&Y. "Anything Neil Young walks into is different thereafter," said Crosby. "I don't care if it's a bathroom." What he brought to the band, his manager said, was "an intensity no-one else could muster".

The Woodstock performance that made them instant superstars was only their second gig together. Slotted between The Butterfield Blues Band and Blood Sweat & Tears on the same day that Hendrix played, CSN&Y were nervous. Young felt particularly uncomfortable. No fan of festivals – he had refused to play Monterey

Pop, of course, with the Springfield; his new bandmate David Crosby, ironically, had stood in for him – he claimed to have only agreed to appear at the biggest alternative youth event of the decade because "I thought it was going to be a joke ... But I wasn't really into it." This was partly for musical reasons ("I could hardly hear myself when we were playing and I didn't know if the people could hear us") and partly for philosophical ones. The gulf that separated him from the half a million or more of his generation, stretched out as far as the eye could see, applied just as much to his outsider status with Crosby, Stills and Nash. As was always the case, it was a self-imposed separateness, something both in-built – as a Canadian in the United States he was never quite part of the club – and learned, a self-defence mechanism to cope with being a child of divorce or with the epilepsy that required a high degree of calm and self-control.

He was "an add-on", he emphasised. "I really didn't want to be just grouped in with a bunch of people even if I thought they were great." Before he agreed to join the band he "made it clear to both sides that I belong to myself". CS&N played a Y-less set before Young came out on-stage to join them; viewers of the Woodstock film would be forgiven for thinking he hadn't joined them at all. The reason Young gave recently for his refusal to be filmed – "To me it was a distraction because music is something that you listen to, not that you look at. You're there, you're playing and you're trying to get lost in the music and there's this dickhead with a camera right in your face. So the only way to make sure that wouldn't happen is to tell then that I wouldn't be in the film" – did not quite ring true, coming from a man who would make several concert movies himself and record on film or video the majority of his shows. A more credible explanation was, "I was the only person in Crosby, Stills, Nash & Young who was, you know, not Crosby, Stills and Nash." While the others would refer to the festival as the zenith of the spirit of the '60s, for Young its only highlights were hearing Jimi Hendrix playing The Star Spangled Banner and driving a stolen pick-up truck around the helicopter landing-field with the guitarist clinging to the bonnet.

"I'm a hack compared to him, a *hack*. That guy – it slipped off his hands," Young raved. "He couldn't help himself. I've got to go in there and hack away with a machete to get through what he just walked through. I can aspire to be able to play that way and to approach it and I'd get halfway there sometimes. I've got a lot of emotion but very little technical ability; Jimi had them both. He can't be touched." Hendrix died, choking on his own barbiturate-laden vomit, just six months after the March '70 release of CSN&Y's debut album, *Déjà Vu*.

If making albums with the Springfield had been arduous, with CSN&Y it was even more so: four singers, writers and producers, two of them in the throes of depression – Crosby because his girlfriend Christine had been killed in a car accident; Nash because his relationship with Crosby's ex-girlfriend Joni Mitchell had just broken up. Stills, whose love life was also blighted, was making plans to decamp to England and play the English squire in the Surrey mansion he was buying from Ringo Starr. Young, meanwhile, was not letting his new band get in the way of writing songs for a solo album. He was also back working with his old band Crazy Horse – leaving the studio where he'd worked with one to head off to another studio to work with the other. "I start off real well, depending on which one I see first," he said. "By the time the day's over I'm just completely screwed up." When it came to the CSN&Y album he preferred to work in the studio alone, sick of the cocaine-fuelled atmosphere and of being outvoted on his attempts to replace their polished perfectionism with his favoured live, no-overdubs approach. None of this, however, had an adverse effect on his contributions to *Déjà Vu*; his two songs Country Girl and Helpless were sublime, the latter an achingly beautiful treatment of the recurrent Young themes of nostalgia, geography, fatalism and the loss of innocence.

Déjà Vu was an enormous hit, shipping gold on advance orders alone. As the band continued to tour the States it topped the charts, going on to sell seven million copies. (In the UK, where they only managed to play the one date at London's Royal Albert Hall, it still charted at a respectable Number 5.) The first single, Woodstock – a cover of Joni Mitchell's festival theme – was predictably a US hit. So was its far superior follow-up, Ohio – Young's tense, emotional tribute to the Kent State University student protesters shot dead by the National Guard; the band took a break from the tour to go into the studio and record it. On the back of CSN&Y's popularity, Young even had a single from his own album, *Everybody Knows This Is Nowhere*, in the charts – Cinammon Girl.

But success had never been a criterion for Young in deciding whether or not to stay with a band. The cracks started to show in CSN&Y even more quickly than they had in The Buffalo Springfield, and by August '70 they had reached crisis point. Young again was the first to bail, leaving for England with Elliot Roberts. He'd planned on making a guest appearance at the Isle Of Wight Festival – solo; he'd broken up with Crazy Horse as well. After playing some shows with them earlier in the year he swore he would never work with them again. Danny Whitten's heroin problem was getting worse. Not that CSN&Y were pharmaceutical-free – Stills had just been arrested on drugs charges after hotel guests found him on his hands and knees jabbering in the corridor. For that matter, Young didn't make it to the Isle Of Wight because customs officers at Heathrow allegedly found some suspicious substances in Elliot Roberts's suitcase, necessitating an instant flight back home. There was plenty to do there anyhow: Young had a new solo album ready for release and was planning on following it with his first major film.

6 The Spirit Of Topanga

WHEN DEAN STOCKWELL, YOUNG'S ACTOR friend and neighbour, showed him the script he'd written for a disaster movie called *After The Gold Rush*, its plot revolving around an innocent folk singer, an earthquake and a freak wave flooding the Canyon, Young immediately asked to direct it and appear in it. The pair hit the film studios in search of financial backing for the film Young described as up there with Easy Rider as a culture-definer, but they drew a blank. "It was too much of an art project," said Young. With the project shelved for the foreseeable future, he borrowed its title for his third solo album.

He had premiered several of its songs on the CSN&Y tour, with Southern Man proving particularly popular. Except with Southern rockers Lynyrd Skynyrd, who wrote Sweet Home Alabama in response. Young wrote it back on The Buffalo Springfield's final tour of the American South, opening for The Beach Boys. Beach Boy percussionist Dennis Dragon recalled, "After one of the shows we went to eat in a diner, me, my brother and Neil. There were some guys sitting across the way who were looking at us with our long hair and we overheard them saying, 'Now you take the one with the curly hair and I'll take the other one and we'll do 'em up'. They were planning to beat us up when we got out of the place – it was straight out of a movie, but it was real. Fortunately some of the other guys arrived and we waited it out and nothing happened, but Neil was really upset – just the vibration, the ignorance, the stupidity; he's a very sensitive guy. That did it. He went straight to work writing Southern Man."

Other songs, according to producer David Briggs, "were written on the spot", including the title track which took half an hour. "Neil would sit upstairs in the living room and then we'd all go downstairs to the basement, turn on the tapes and away we'd go." This way they recorded almost all of the album live in the home studio Young had constructed earlier that year. If you had good enough ears and equipment you could apparently hear the sound of his dogs barking outside in the yard. The album, Young said, captured "the spirit of Topanga Canyon".

Crazy Horse had been augmented by Greg Reeves – and Stills – from CSN&Y, Young's old friend Jack Nitzsche and new recruit Nils Lofgren, whom they'd met backstage at the Cellar Door club in Washington DC when they played there the year before. Ralph Molina recalls, "This kid walks in the dressing room who's like 16 or 17, all jacked up with his guitar, and Danny told him, 'Come on out to California.' And in two weeks he came out," bringing his unsigned band Grin with him. Briggs took them under his wing. "We got back from the tour and Neil liked him, we liked him, and then Neil asked him to play on *After The Gold Rush*."

The album's gentle melodicism was in stark contrast to *Everybody Knows This Is Nowhere*, but once again its love songs spoke of disillusion, confusion and loss.

Despite acknowledging his wife Susan (for the wifely task of having sewn the nice patches on his jeans) for the first time in the credits, and having what appears on the sleeve photo a crone-like conjoined twin growing out of his back, the words he sang in a voice like a human pedal steel painted the picture of an introspective loner. There was even a mournful cover of the old country song Oh Lonesome Me. The image he'd acquired from his debut album as a kind of long-haired, counter-culture Roy Orbison would be as good as set in stone, as the album vied with James Taylor's *Sweet Baby James* as *the* bedsit album of the year.

Girls dug it. Which is probably why so many rock critics bristled. "Neil Young devotees will probably spend the next few weeks desperately trying to convince themselves that *After The Gold Rush* is good music. But they'll be kidding themselves. None of the songs rises above the uniformly dull surface" was how Rolling Stone reviewed one of Young's most appealing and enduring records (although NME's annual poll voted him Best Vocalist and Melody Maker elected *Gold Rush* their Album Of The Year). His second huge hit album of 1970, Top 10 in the US and UK, it made Young one of the record business's hottest properties. Not a bad way to start a new decade – if it hadn't been for the dissolving marriage and disintegrating spine.

While he was on the road with CSN&Y, Young heard about a ranch and land for sale in a secluded, woody area an hour's drive south of San Francisco. When the tour hit northern California he went to see it and bought it with the proceeds from *Déjà Vu*. As with his Topanga house, as soon as the tour was over he set to fixing it up, and in doing so slipped a disc. He wore a surgical back-brace to play his residency at the Cellar Door and his year-end shows at the prestigious Carnegie Hall. They were seated acoustic shows – standing for long was impossible and playing electric guitar hurt like hell. There was a good reason for not staying at home and having his wife take care of him: Neil and Susan had broken up.

The problem with relationships, he had once told his father when trying to explain his break-up with Robin Lane, was that "too often when I got home I picked up the guitar instead of the girl". The problem with Susan was that he rarely got home; with his career on a roll, he was almost constantly on the road, either alone or with Crazy Horse or CSN&Y. In the rare moments when he was there, all he wanted was peace and quiet and wifely looking-after, but the house would be filled with the people that kept his wife company while he was gone. Young thought of most of them as "parasites" – leftover '60s freeloaders and '70s rock-star hangers-on.

Whatever its cause, their divorce was as sudden as their marriage had been. By the end of the year Susan and her daughter had slipped out of the Topanga house and into obscurity, where she has remained ever since. Young made one of his very rare public statements about the marriage in a VH1 documentary 30 years later: "Susan, my first wife, was a wonderful lady. She was older than I was, and I really wasn't grown up enough for her. It took me a long time to grow up because all my growing-up time was spent on music. All the other things suffered for it." Right then he was certainly suffering once again in the health department, but emotionally things weren't so bad: he was in a new relationship already with the film actress Carrie Snodgress.

*

The back problem was serious – degenerated discs that required surgery. For the first time since leaving Canada five years earlier – during which time he had made eight albums (including the Springfield retrospective) with three bands, five of them hits – Young was forced to rest. He was sitting around at the house watching TV with a friend when he fell in love with the actress in the movie Diary Of A Mad Housewife. The part she played that Young said he could understand was of a rebellious young woman trapped in a suffocating marriage to a lawyer; love makes empathists of us all. Getting her phone number from another friend, he called her up, and they arranged to meet after his operation. Jumping the gun, Snodgress showed up at his hospital bed.

The relationship became intense quickly, as Young's strongest relationships, musical or otherwise, always did. The cut in his tour schedule ordered by the doctors gave it more time than usual to develop. Not that a man with such an intrinsic need to keep moving would take instructions to stay put too literally; having completed his scheduled US solo tour he even managed to fly to London in February '71, traction machine in tow, for two performances: a BBC TV broadcast and a concert at the Royal Festival Hall. "Uproar Over Sell-Out" screamed the headlines as the South Bank's booking office was jammed with calls from desperate fans. "Patricia Wragg, a young switchboard operator, was almost reduced to tears," the newspaper reported, "following abusive phone calls from callers complaining they were unable to get tickets." There was another reason for the visit: Young had hired the London World Symphony Orchestra to play on two of his new songs – A Man Needs A Maid, inspired by Snodgress, and the ominous-sounding There's A World. Jack Nitzsche, who wrote their extravagant orchestral arrangements, flew in to conduct, in the somewhat less than grandiose setting of Barking Town Hall in East London.

Although Young had been asked to leave the flat he rented in London for making too much noise, back at the ranch – where Carrie had moved in to join him – and still in considerable pain, he had no choice but to become laid-back. Often unable to move and under sedation, he would have to play the new songs that he was writing gently, on an acoustic guitar, since he was too weak to play an electric one. He decided he would start recording them on his upcoming trip to Nashville. He had been invited by country star Johnny Cash to appear on his weekly TV show: "I told them I wouldn't do a show unless I could bring in every kind of music that the people wanted to see and hear, because television was for everybody, so I managed to bring in quite a few rock stars," said Cash. "I really liked Neil – he was real country and very intense – so I had him on my show twice." James Taylor and Young's old Topanga neighbour Linda Ronstadt were on the programme too – since Bob Dylan's duet with Cash on Bob's 1969 album *Nashville Skyline*, which he recorded in Nashville, country music had lost at least some of its reputation as unforgivably conservative and reactionary – and when shooting was done Young took them with him into Quadrafonic Studios.

Finding musicians in Nashville wasn't difficult. "As I understand it," said Ben Keith, "Tim [Drummond, bass player] was just walking by and they came right out and got him. They asked if he knew of a steel guitar player and I lived right up the block so he called me up. When I came down the session was actually already going; I quietly snuck in there and started playing. We cut three or four songs without stopping – Harvest and Heart Of Gold and some others – before we even met. Neil liked to do everything live – if something didn't work right away he would leave it and maybe try it another day." When they finally took a breather, Young made Keith an official member of the new band he dubbed The Stray Gators, which also included Drummond, drummer Kenny Buttrey and Jack Nitzsche.

"I knew of CSN&Y," said Keith, "though I didn't know that he'd done a solo album, but I thought he was great. I knew it was going to be something different from anything I'd ever heard. He liked to switch around and work in different places when he was looking for different sounds, so we went out to his ranch and continued recording there – Words, Alabama, Are You Ready For The Country. We played in the old barn that's pictured on the back of the album – we did some real nice stuff there – with 600 ft of line out into his valley, which we used for an echo-chamber on those tracks. You could hear it for miles."

Meanwhile, in April '71 *4 Way Street*, the posthumous CSN&Y live double album compiled from the last tour by Graham Nash, hit the shops and Young found himself with another enormous hit – Number 1 in the US and Number 5 in the UK. But his solo album *Harvest* would do better still: a chart-topper on both sides of the Atlantic. The sing-along hit single Heart Of Gold made him a household name. "It can only be concluded," wrote Rolling Stone, which had praised *4 Way Street* to the skies, "that Neil Young is not one of those folks whom superstardom becomes artistically." The magazine accused him of "invoking most of the LA variety of superstardom's weariest clichés in an attempt to obscure his ability to do a good imitation of his earlier self". NME agreed: *Harvest* was "excruciatingly dull", it said. "Like so many of his contemporaries he was now reduced to parodying his past successes in even grander circumstances."

Admittedly his circumstances were pretty grand for a 27-year-old, if less ostentatious than other superstars who hadn't snorted up all their income (the lake dominated by two outdoor stereo speakers the size of a house so he could listen to music from a rowing boat in the middle; the black-tiled hill-top swimming pool for exercising his back muscles in). And, true, his pastoral new album did not dig too deeply into the darkest reaches of his soul, but it didn't deserve such excoriation. Although this writer would be happy to never again hear the sappy Heart Of Gold (and still winces at the lyrics and overwrought orchestration of A Man Needs A Maid), the subdued passion of The Needle And The Damage Done, the emotional fragility of Old Man and the dreaminess of the harmonica, guitar and pedal steel on Out On The Weekend guaranteed it a place in the collection.

"I was saying OK, let's just get really, really mellow and peaceful, make music that's just as intense as the electric stuff but which comes from a completely different . . . more loving place," Young explained about the calm before one of his violent electric storms. But some people – the ones who helped make *Harvest* his best-selling album ever – simply heard him saying he was a down-home, laid-back, country-loving, California hippie.

LIFE, DEATH AND CUERVO GOLD: THE DOOM TRILOGY

7 The Horror, The Horror.

*It's not like the art is separate from the life, it's one
and the same with Neil.*

Elliot Roberts

A NARROW ROAD LED THROUGH THE WOODS
high off the sequoia-lined Skyline Boulevard towards
Young's rustic sanctuary, midway between San Francisco
and Santa Cruz. Broken Arrow ranch's 140 acres, looking
out over Half Moon Bay, had a duck pond, a lake, a hilltop
pool, horses, dogs, corrals, old buildings, one of them
turned into a studio, and a house with smoke curling
out of the chimney, where Young's new partner, Carrie

Snodgress, nursed their two-month-old son Zeke. Some successful rock stars upgrade their cars or their drugs supply; Young appeared to have upgraded his Topanga Canyon domestic idyll with Susan and her little girl.

A more agreeable spot to sit out the short space of time that separated Heart Of Gold and the heart of darkness would be hard to find. It was November '72. *Harvest* was shaping up as the year's biggest-selling album; Zeke's cerebral palsy had not yet been diagnosed; Carrie, like the maid the man said he needed, had revealed in an interview she would be putting her acting career on hold to take care of Neil and the baby; and Young – who had just celebrated his 27th birthday – was sufficiently up and about from his back problems to be contemplating his first major tour in 18 months. Which was why his old friend Jack Nitzsche and the *Harvest* musicians were on their way up to the ranch to rehearse.

As an afterthought, Neil got on the phone to Danny Whitten, the guitarist he'd fired in May 1970 – the rest of Crazy Horse along with him – for being too fucked up to play. Perhaps he wanted to share his good fortune with a friend; perhaps his back, or the long gap between tours, had left him insecure as a guitar player; perhaps, with all those Nashville pros around, he wanted someone as sensitive and intense as he was along for the ride (if not quite as intense as Nitzsche). Whitten swore to him that he was no longer on smack. What he'd failed to mention was that he was on just about anything else he could get. It was painfully obvious on arrival that he was in a similar state to the previous year's sessions for Crazy Horse's debut album when Nils Lofgren, brought in as back-up, had to tune his instrument for him: the guitar player equivalent of having someone wipe your butt.

"He had trouble remembering the lines and the lyrics," recalled Ben Keith. "He just couldn't remember from day to day. We tried very hard – a week or two." But eventually Young had to face it: Danny was "too far gone". He fired him again. The guitarist pleaded to stay; told him he had "nowhere else to go". They took him to the airport, gave him $50 and put him on the plane back home – where he immediately blew the $50 on heroin. That same night, while Young and the band were rehearsing, there was a phone call from the LA county coroner. Whitten had fatally OD'd.

In spite – or because – of *Harvest*'s huge success, Young was already acquiring an almost Conradian take on rock stardom as a diseased and malevolent black hole sucking all joy and vitality out of anyone who got too close. Young, who knew a lot about sickness, had taken steps early on to immunise himself from its excesses. He had indulged in the Buffalo Springfield groupie scene, but only to a limited degree, before marrying an older woman – someone stable, with a child, who had run a café – to look after him. Although Graham Nash claimed that they "all got into drugs seriously", Young's epilepsy had ensured his avoidance of anything much stronger than pot. And when the money started coming in, like the good chicken farmer he'd always wanted to be, he carefully counted his eggs and put some aside for the future: the cheque from his solo record deal had gone straight into buying the house in Topanga, just as his income from CSN&Y had paid for Broken Arrow ranch.

With *Harvest* topping the charts on both sides of the Atlantic, it seemed the more Young got what he'd wanted from the music business, the less contented he felt. Having a Number 1 single with Heart Of Gold was "empty". Quite how he found being filed alongside James Taylor in California's fuck-me-I'm-sensitive singer-songwriters school can only be imagined. The mainstream press embraced him (The Spectator: "Of all the narcissists from California's West Coast he is the most approachable. Young's songs have a pliable compassion about them, a summery, fernlike quality which is balm on the eyelids and sunflowers in the ears"), while the rock press accused him of dumbing down and selling out. "I thought the record was good," said Young, "but I also knew that something else was dying."

Out in his isolated mountain home, cut off by choice and temperament from friends and associates – the Springfield, Crazy Horse, CS&N – and having recently gone through divorce, operations and fatherhood, the big black hole was sucking away stronger than ever. "Neil loved Danny," said Ralph Molina. He was the first of The Rockets he'd met; he was the one who had encouraged Neil – still insecure about his voice in the Springfield days – to sing. And, in the way that his close friendships seemed indivisible from his music, Young's despondency at his friend's heroin death was inextricably linked with anger at being denied the chance of watching his musical relationship with Danny and Crazy Horse develop.

"We thought we had it with Danny Whitten," said Young in '75. "At least I did. I thought that I had a combination of people that could be as effective as groups like The Rolling Stones had been – just for rhythm, which I'm really into . . . I've had to play the rhythm myself ever since Danny died." That call from the coroner "fucking blew my mind . . . I felt responsible . . . And from there I had to go right out on this huge tour . . ."

The good news was that the 60-plus shows were a sell-out. The bad news was they were arenas (Young was "nervous and not quite at home in those big places"). The even worse news was that the band and crew were demanding more money and a share of the profits; the road manager was set to quit halfway through; and drummer Ken Buttrey, stressed out from all the arguing, was to follow. Camaraderie was zero. Even the mild-mannered Ben Keith's memories are that "It was really rough." Betrayed, cornered, his nerves shot with Danny's death and drinking heavily, Young met their demands, inwardly seething, particularly as he felt that "the band without Danny Whitten wasn't making it." He might well have seethed outwardly if the nodes in his throat weren't getting so bad that it hurt to talk. Which only added to a sense of isolation already compounded by the crowd who, lured by the chart-topping *Harvest*, were expecting a laid-back country hippie, not this grim man in a work-shirt snarling at them for making too much noise during the fragile acoustic numbers and not enough during the corrosive new electric ones, while they waited for him to play Heart Of Gold. He could have made it easy for himself, of course, and given them the eyelid-balm and aural sunflowers they'd come for; instead he continued to add new, sometimes corrosively savage material. "Neil was coming up with new things all the time," recalled *Harvest* producer Elliot Mazer, who recorded the tour. "There were always new things to do and rehearse."

Reviewers were a little more kind about the shows than they'd been about Young's double soundtrack album *Journey Through The Past* (its pre-Christmas – not to mention pre-film – release had been his record company's idea, payment for bankrolling its distribution). But that was hardly difficult, seeing that *Journey* had been written off as "self-indulgent, frustrating, unworthy . . . a ragbag collection of old Buffalo Springfield and CSN&Y live cuts and tapes from the *Harvest* session seemingly salvaged from the cutting room floor" (Melody Maker) and "the nadir of NY's recording activity. Whether the existence of any film could justify the existence of this record is questionable" (Rolling Stone).

As was, and would often be, the case, when the strain of being in the front seat got too much, Young's gaze would turn towards Crosby Stills & Nash. "He said it wasn't going very well and that he needed our help," said Crosby, who answered the emergency call with Nash (Stills being busy getting married), joining the beleaguered tour when it hit the West Coast. They stuck around to offer as much cheer as a man whose mother was dying of cancer (Crosby) and whose girlfriend had just been murdered by her brother (Nash) could muster as the tour limped through the final dates to its grim conclusion at the Oakland Coliseum. Midway through Southern Man, as an enthusiastic fan leapt from his seat to cheer its anti-racist message, a black cop "just ran up and smashed this guy down", said Young. "It was like I was watching myself on TV and someone had pulled out the plug. I was playing on, but I couldn't believe what I'd just seen. I was disconnected. Then I got out of that place and I said to myself, who *needs* it? Who needs to be a dot in the distance for 20,000 people and give the cops another excuse to get uptight and stop kids being happy. I'm tired of singing to a cop, that's all."

Of course it wasn't all, but it was a good enough reason anyhow to cancel the European tour. Instead he flew to Dallas where *Journey Through The Past* was being premiered at a film festival. The crowds who cheered Young's name in the opening credits weren't quite so spirited by the screening's end, but unfazed, or simply battleworn, Young stuck around to conduct a Q&A session. As he said later, "Once in a while I like to do something that has a chance of failing." A curious sentiment from a man who'd always shown such a grim determination to succeed. Except his determination that his audience shouldn't think they'd got him sussed was grimmer still.

The support offered by Crosby and Nash when he needed it warmed Young to the idea of taking a break from his solo career and submerging himself in a CSN&Y record. The four arranged to meet up early in the summer on the Hawaiian island of Maui, where Nash had rented them a house and Crosby had moored his boat. Work started on an album to be titled *Human Highway*, but before long the band were at one another's throats. It was not something that Young – who'd already had a surgeon at his throat a month earlier, cutting out the nodes that had plagued him on tour – was willing to suffer. He packed his bags and flew home.

Jack Nitzsche, with whom Young had fallen out on tour, had claimed that "Neil's whole lifestyle is that of the millionaire who doesn't give a shit about anybody but himself", but photos shot at Broken Arrow that summer of '73 told a different story. With his lank hair, pale face and tormented eyes, the man clutching his guitar and glaring murderously at the lens looked anything but a wealthy, smug, contented rock star. On his return, Young had just learned that another of his friends had taken a fatal overdose: guitar roadie Bruce Berry.

When CS&N turned up at the ranch in search of a second chance with their missing letter, Young was not in the mood for the egos and the petty squabbling that soon broke out. On his way to the studio barn he turned tail and drove to David Briggs' house – they were once again neighbours, since Briggs had moved down from Canada where he had been running a studio. "I was on my way to a CSN&Y session," he said, "and I just don't feel like going there. Let's make some rock'n'roll." So they threw some stuff in the car and took off to Los Angeles, where they gathered up the remains of Crazy Horse.

It had been three years since Molina and Talbot had been ditched along with Danny Whitten, but they answered Neil's call, as they always did. Adding Nils Lofgren and Ben Keith, the newly dubbed Santa Monica Flyers went through their paces in two shows at Young's old stomping ground, the Topanga Corral. Recalled Ben Keith: "It was just like a garage band that got together and went into a garage and played – it was a small place, around 200 people. We were just having fun."

Afterwards they booked a room at SIR – the rehearsal studios on the corner of Hollywood's Vine Street and Santa Monica Boulevard owned by Bruce Berry's brother Ken (another brother was Jan of Jan &

Dean). Here, with the help of a mobile recording truck and several cases of Cuervo Gold tequila, they recorded three quarters of one of the starkest, most bleakly beautiful rock albums ever made: *Tonight's The Night*.

"The room was the size of a small nightclub with couches at one end and the stage at the other. I remember thinking that it was a strange decision to record there. This was a rehearsal hall. There were many other bands rehearsing at the time," recalled Bruce Gary, who was in one of those bands. "The walls were not completely soundproof. The vibe was as spooky as the album sounds. It was *very* loud, and endless – they had the room block-booked and didn't leave until they had everything they wanted on tape. There was a lot of booze consumed. I remember Briggs running back and forth between the room and the mobile recording truck. I hung out until I couldn't take it anymore."

On the small folded sheet of paper tucked inside the album, looking with its pictures of Roy Orbison, Huckleberry Finn, a speeding car and Cuervo Gold like a prayer-card to some particularly *outré* Catholic saint, was a photocopy of an article by a Dutch writer that explained what the whole business was about. The fact that it was written in Dutch, and so few of Young's fans would have the faintest idea what was going on, was fine with Young, who didn't understand what was going on himself. His own sleevenotes – a stoned stream-of-consciousness letter addressed to "Waterface", and the rambling lyrics of his still-unreleased song Florida about a crashed glider, a dead couple and a baby – made just as much sense. Except for the epigraph: "This album was made for Danny Whitten and Bruce Berry, who lived and died for rock and roll." Technically, they died for heroin, but this was a time when rock was conjoined at the head and hip with drugs and sex. Young's failure to fully embrace the drugs counter-culture of late '60s/early '70s California was as unusual for a rock star as his relative lack of satyriasis during the Summer of Love. A lot of people, of course, thought Young was a junkie, thanks in part to his epileptic habit of collapsing on-stage, but "I wouldn't go anywhere near that stuff," he said, "not even snorting it." Whitten on the other hand "didn't snort nothing", according to his friend Billy Talbot. "He just shot some speed, the next day some smack, and from then on he was a junkie."

Ralph Molina: "There was one point where Danny went into a hospital and then he left and came and stayed with us for a while. But he was like really far gone. I mean, he tried the cure and he didn't do it. He got into the methadone thing and he started drinking a lot of wine. He got real heavy – he couldn't make it through rehearsal."

Nils Lofgren: "After I helped make the first Crazy Horse album, Danny Whitten came back to Maryland with me and was going to join Grin, but at this point it became clear to me how sick he was, and he went back to California and died not long afterwards. I think, with *Tonight's The Night*, even though it was a dark record with a lot of frustration and anger, rather than sit around and mope about Danny's and Bruce Berry's death, we all purged ourselves by making that album. I think in a strange way we all had a case of the 'fuck its'. It wasn't that morose. We'd show up at SIR at five or six in the afternoon, just played pool, partied, visited, commiserated."

Molina: "Sometimes you didn't get out until six in the morning. Neil was so into it – we were all into it. It was like a family thing. It was great. The emotion was just dripping" – helped no doubt by the alarming amounts of alcohol and weed consumed over the loud late-night sessions-cum-wakes.

Young: "We were spooked. Right out on the edge . . . We knew it was different when we were doing it – everything live, everybody playing and singing at the same time, the way the old blues people used to do it."

Lofgren: "We'd jam, play and record in this very bare-bones fashion. Neil was clear that his intent was to let people see how a record is before it gets all polished and nice. I remember Ralph and I constantly asking Neil if we could fix this or that little part and he'd say, no, he wanted it just as it was."

Young: "Sometimes I'd be on the mic, sometimes I'd be two feet off it . . . I can remember the first time I heard it I said, 'That's the most out-of-tune thing I've ever done.'"

Bleak and cathartic, its wasted vocals and ragged production were the antithesis of the consumer-friendly *Harvest*. Definitely not the album his record company had in mind, especially on the tail of a panned film, a panned soundtrack album and a panned tour on which Young had been downright hostile towards the audience. Asked what his fans would make of this, he shrugged, "It's real. Either you'll want to hear it or you won't."

They might have been able to stop its release; they couldn't stop him going out and playing the songs live. Weeks later, a dishevelled Young, wearing a white jacket and sunglasses, stumbled on-stage at the Roxy – David Geffen's new 500-seater rock nightclub bought as a rival to the Whisky down the Strip. Elliot Roberts, who was now Geffen's partner in a management business, was a part-owner of the club, and their client's four-night stand would be its opening performances. The Santa Monica Flyers shared the stage with a palm tree, a wooden cigarette store Indian, an old piano, a bunch of silver glitter boots and a fair old amount of tequila; Young would drink – and belch – openly. During one set he insisted (to Geffen's evident displeasure) on free drinks for the audience; during another he offered the prize of a boot to any woman willing to come on-stage with her top off (Carrie Snodgress won). Part theatre, part catharsis, part cryptic black joke, the shows had people wondering whether Young was burned out, junked up, or barking mad. By the time the Chinese whispers crossed the Atlantic they'd grown into reports that the singer had OD'd.

NME, October 1973: "A weird rumour has been sweeping London like wildfire to the effect that Neil Young was dead and that drugs were the cause. The rumour seems to have started in the States and gained hold with such rapidity that his record company had actually started an obituary."

The following month – a year now since Danny Whitten's death – the Tonight's The Night tour rolled into Britain. It was much the same as the Roxy show except the free drinks and topless Carrie were replaced with The Eagles, chosen more one imagines because they were Geffen-Roberts stablemates than as a sunny counterbalance to Young's wild, jagged gloom. "Neil was sort of dribbling out of the side of his mouth on that tour," recalled Elliot Roberts. "The mood was so down."

Lofgren: "Throughout the tour I'd wear these heavy combat boots and ankle weights because the music was so slow and plodding that I needed them to sink down into the groove of the songs. Although Neil wasn't playing so much guitar on that tour, there were moments where there would be some very fierce interplay between the piano and guitar, eventually ending in a crescendo of chaos. On Tonight's The Night, Neil would start pounding on the piano and going into these insane raps off the top of his head – raps about Bruce Berry and sticking guitars in your arm – and I'd wind up on top of the piano. When I'd switch to piano for other songs I'd play this very melodic honky-tonk, almost countryesque style and Neil would play these thick chords on his old black Les Paul, and we'd marry those to Ben Keith's beautiful, bizarre steel. It was a haunting sound with a lot of anger and bite in it."

The fans, like many of the critics, did not know what to think, having no idea of the provenance of this furiously downbeat, fucked-up music, with slurred monologues about dead people and Miami Beach, Richard Nixon masks and theatrical goings-on. "It's good for them," shrugged Young. "Better that than something they understand."

"I paid £2.50 to see Neil Young at the Rainbow on Nov 5 and came away with a love-hate relationship: hating

Neil Young but loving The Eagles," a fan wrote to Melody Maker's letters page, echoing several of the press reviews. "It wasn't that the audience were hostile. On the contrary everybody wanted to love him. He just refused to give the audience what they wanted. There was no Ohio, no Southern Man, only a mediocre version of Helpless and Cowgirl In The Sand, which turned into an ego trip for all concerned. All I can say is the rumours must be true: the real Neil Young is dead."

Lofgren: "All the English fans looked at Neil as this dark, brooding god. The audience in general was freaking out that Neil wouldn't play any of his old hits. He was trying to turn them on to something, which he's always done, but this was an extreme example of that. There were a couple of nights where the audience was so rude that Neil finally stormed off-stage, really upset. One night he came storming out and launched without telling us into a 15-minute, searing version of Down By The River, which was basically Neil's way of saying, 'Is that what you want?'"

It was a dark tour, Lofgren said, but added, "We all had a sense of humour about it." By the tour's end he was describing it as "fun". "We had a ball," said Ben Keith; Young would call it "fabulous; one of my best ever". Endless repetition of a problem – as anyone who's been anywhere near a therapist knows – eventually dulls its pain; by telling the story of his friends' destruction over and over, night after night, Young had effectively distanced himself from the torment. The whacked-out, mumbling frontman had become an act, another mask he could hide behind to provoke the fans.

Not everyone at the UK shows walked out or stared in incomprehension. Sid Vicious, interviewed on the Sex Pistols' American tour, claimed to have been at the Manchester show and said that the raw, abrasive music and Young's goading of the audience had been a major influence. Other future punks would say the same thing to Neil. "Not that I'm saying they eventually based their trip on us, by any stretch of the imagination," he said years later, "but they did remember . . ."

8 A Wart On The Perfect Beast

THE POSTERS THAT PAPERED THE WALLS OF the venues along the Autumn '73 UK tour announced the release of Young's new album. Not the tense, bleak new material he had been playing live with the Santa Monica Flyers, but the tense, nihilistic new material he'd played – and recorded – live with the Stray Gators on the tour from hell: *Time Fades Away*.

Asked, decades later, what was the worst album he had ever made, Young answered, "Probably *Time Fades Away*. But only because it makes me so nervous. That whole tour was a nervous experience. I kind of got into documenting that vibe. It's not something I want to listen to a lot. It makes you feel uneasy. The only redeeming factor was that it truly reflected where I was at." Messy, dislocated, claustrophobic, it captured perfectly the atmosphere of the tour and the turmoil of Young's inner life. It would be the first of three-in-a-row dark, confused, revelatory albums. The so-called Doom Trilogy reflected not only Young's dark night of the soul but his determination, post-*Harvest*, not to give the Melody Maker letter-writer and his like what they wanted him to give them. By becoming their performing dog, "They would have thought that they understood what I was all about and that would have been it for me," he explained. "I would have painted myself in the corner. The fact is I'm not that lone, laid-back figure with a guitar. I'm just not that way anymore. I'd rather keep changing and lose a lot of people along the way. If that's the price, I'll pay it. I don't give a shit if my audience is a hundred or a hundred million . . . I'm convinced that what sells and what I do are two completely different things. If they meet, it's coincidence."

Sometimes, of course, what he said and what he did were also two completely different things. On the

Time Fades Away arena tour, having collided head-on with the Great Rock Paradox – artist whose intimate music appeals to a large number of people must, in order to satisfy their desire for personal contact, play ever-larger, more impersonal, less intimate venues – Young had detested being "a dot in the distance for 20,000 people". Then in March '74, news broke that Crosby, Stills, Nash & Young were rehearsing at Young's ranch (where he'd had a 40 ft outdoor stage purpose-built) for a summer stadium tour. It was to be a real juggernaut, with all the pomp, excess, cocaine and decadence that mid-'70s rock money could buy – which, with the growth of the recording industry, was a shitload. Though not even Led Zeppelin had insisted on having custom-made pillowcases on every hotel bed. CSN&Y's bed-linen sported a silk-screened tour logo painted by Joni Mitchell. They had a pair of Lear jets. While they grappled with the problem of dividing up who would fly in which, Young went by road in a bus. "He loves driving down the old highway," said Crosby.

Having agreed to the tour, he'd bought an old rig he'd dubbed the Buffalo Springfield. He customised it with observation towers in the roof made out of the tops of two ancient Buick Roadmasters and built a galley kitchen, redwood cupboards and beds, turning it into a mobile home. Travelling with him were a roadie, Art the dog, and sometimes Zeke and Carrie, all – dog included – sporting-access-all-areas passes. The tour started well, but before long it was heading decidedly Spinal Tapwards, with Young and Stills – even Crosby with his 12-string acoustic – upping the amps to 11 to drown the others out. And Young's colleagues weren't all taking too kindly to some of the dark new material he'd added to the set – Revolution Blues for instance, a real summer bummer inspired by his old pal Charlie Manson. It came from Young's new album recorded prior to, and released midway through, the CSN&Y stadium tour. *On The Beach* was, said Young, "like a wart or something on the perfect beast".

On The Beach, said NME's review of the album recorded on a diet of "honey-slides" (hash melted in honey; he'd shared the recipe with the Rainbow crowd on the Tonight's The Night tour) "is whichever way you look at it a depression record. A downer in that depression is the mood which most of the album evokes. But also depressing because Neil Young isn't writing as well as he used to . . . He sounds consecutively bitter, hopeless, cynical and world-weary." Melody Maker concurred: "The melancholia has given way to stifling depression, the sensitivity replaced by self-pity and world-weariness . . . and oppressive sense of despondency." Which didn't quite tie in with the waggish, self-mocking sleeve photo, non-sleevenote sleevenotes and flashes of cynical black humour and optimism in the lyrics. But true, Young himself told Rolling Stone it was "probably one of the most depressing albums I've made". Three out of eight songs had the word "blues" in the title, its sound was raw, hard, uncompromising, and its themes took in decay, shattered illusions, paranoia, nostalgia, isolation, the downside of fame, the death of the hippie dream, the decline and fall of American culture.

They were wrong about the standard of song-writing, though. The precision with which Young depicts the darkness under the California sun and analyses his place in it is remarkable. The flat silver-grey sea which Young, on the cover photo, stares out into could just as

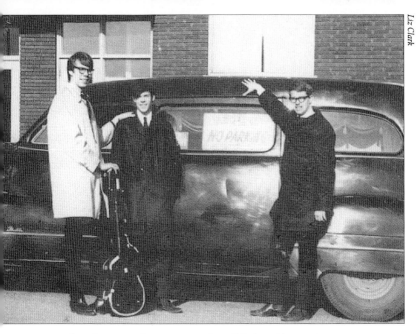

The Fab Four – The Squires and Neil's beloved hearse Mort
L to R: Ken Koblun, Neil Young, Bob Clark

After a failed career modelling knitwear, Young co-founds Buffalo Springfield
L to R: Dewey Martin, Bruce Palmer, Stephen Stills, Richie Furay, Neil Young

Young ponders the state of his solo career – 1969

CSN&Y rehearsing at Stephen Stills's house for their first live show, August 1969

Young and Crazy Horse on the beach, Malibu 1975
L to R: Neil Young, Frank "Poncho" Sampedro, Billy Talbot, Ralph Molina

Charles Manson,
the man who
killed the '60s

Manager
Elliott Roberts
backstage at
the Fillmore
East,
March 1970

A man finds a
maid. Neil
with second
(and current)
wife Pegi

Neil Young going it alone, 1970

Behind the shades, live in the '70

With The Band at *The Last Waltz*

Techno boffin Neil touring Trans, 1982

Live in the '9
the axe-murde

well be a mirror reflecting not just his own image but that created for him by the music business and fans. NME's then assistant editor Ian MacDonald stepped in with a lengthy and insightful reassessment. *On The Beach* – "an album that – for me – seems clearly to be Neil Young's best so far" – wasn't "as previously interpreted, the fag-end of Neil Young's romance with rejection, but actually a quite positive piece of work in the Merciless Realism bracket of Lennon's primal period." The name of Bob Dylan, the third member of rock's triumvirate, was also invoked. "Personally I think Young heard Dylan on tour recently, copped for what the new version of It's Alright Ma was all about ('I've got nothing ma, to live up to') and decided he'd been jerking off too long . . . Though Dylan and Young may have taken a parallel path recently, Young now sounds actively *dangerous* whereas Dylan's just singing his own peculiar gospel," he concluded.

Meanwhile, what the UK press were calling "the tour of the century" (support acts were Joni Mitchell, The Band and Jesse Colin Young) rolled into Wembley Stadium in mid-September for its final show. CSN&Y had had enough of each other by this point; certainly Young seemed to have no more need of "the perfect beast". But neither was he in any hurry to get home. After the show was over, he jammed with Stills and members of The Band and Led Zeppelin on Vampire Blues and On The Beach in a Piccadilly nightclub; and after the party was over he bought himself a 1934 Rolls-Royce in London, christened it "Wembley" and had it shipped off to Amsterdam with the aim of driving it around Europe with Nash and some friends. The car made it to Belgium before it broke down, so Young stuck around there. The alternative was the domestic conflict waiting for him back at Broken Arrow.

Shortly after his return, Carrie and Zeke moved out – as did Neil – upset, as he had been in Topanga, that his sanctuary had been invaded by "parasites" while he was on the road. He moved down south to Zuma Beach, Malibu, where David Briggs had a house. Young's relationship with the actress had "lasted not much longer than Buffalo Springfield", he wrote to his father. "Rock-'n'roll and the life of a musician turn out to be pretty bad for a family. Carrie seeks the simple things that I sing about and have trouble reaching." There had been talk

– then again, there rarely wasn't – of another CSN&Y album, but as with the last time nothing came of it. In his beach-house off the Pacific Coast Highway, Young was working on an album about the break-up of his relationship with Snodgress.

That *Homegrown* was a mainly acoustic album must have delighted his record company. But when in one of his last-minute changes he told them he wanted to release *Tonight's The Night* instead they barely blinked. On the back of his exposure from the CSN&Y stadium tour, they probably thought that anything with Young's name on would sell; *Tonight's The Night* would be better than the nothing they might well get if they refused to play ball (although their confidence in their star's salesworthiness must have wavered a little, since the initial pressing was reportedly small).

Young had made his decision after listening to a tape of *Homegrown* with some friends back-to-back with the tracks recorded at SIR for *Tonight's The Night*; their raw intensity only emphasised *Homegrown*'s failing. But credit for the final appearance of what many, this author included, consider Young's masterpiece should go to those strange, unsung folk behind a prospective but sadly still unstaged Broadway musical based on the life and death of Bruce Berry.

"The plot," said Young, "was about a roadie who made it and then OD'd on drugs. From Roadie To Riches was the name of it. For Broadway in 1974 it was a little ahead of its time . . ." They approached Young's management for some songs, and Elliot and Neil went through the boxes of tapes finding three older, unused songs – Lookout Joe, Borrowed Tune and a live take with Crazy Horse of Come On Baby Let's Go Downtown, Danny Whitten on lead vocals – that would make up the nine recorded at the wake to an album's worth.

The album Young would name on a 1981 US radio show as his most significant ("It's the black sheep of the family; I just like it") was finally released in June 1975 with Young's first-ever press launch party. "I never had an album that you could party to and interview to before," he joked (or not) to the small posse of interviewers. Its delay, he told them, was because it just wasn't in the right space, the right order.

"I had to get the colour right so it was not so down

that it would make people restless," he said. "I had to keep jolting every once in a while to get people to wake up so they could be lulled again." It could almost stand as a statement for his career.

RUST-BUSTER: 1975–79

9 The Return Of The Horse

*Somehow I feel like I've surfaced out of some kind
of murk.*

IN AN EARLY 1975 INTERVIEW WITH CAMERON
Crowe, Young spoke of his excitement at all the new ideas
running around in his brain. The bachelor life suited him.
"This is the first time I can remember coming out of a
relationship definitely not wanting to get into another
one," he said. Even by Young's prolific standards, the
mid-'70s period between leaving Carrie Snodgress and
marrying Pegi Morton was astonishingly productive: in
less than four years that followed the aborted *Homegrown,*

he put out six albums, all quite different – *Tonight's The Night, Zuma, American Stars'N'Bars, Comes A Time, Long May You Run* with Stephen Stills, and his three album retrospective, *Decade.* He also wrote a film, Human Highway, appeared in The Band's film The Last Waltz, and played live in the US, Europe and Japan variously backed by The Stills-Young Band, The Gone With The Wind Orchestra, The Ducks, three wooden cigar-store Indians, and his old band Crazy Horse.

Since the death of Danny Whitten and the depression and heavy drinking that followed was the cause of at least some of the dark cloud that had hung over him since *Harvest*, it went without saying that the return of the Horse would make a hole for the sun to creep through. With Crazy Horse there had always been a solidity, a sense of being a whole. When he first jammed with them, back in the fractious Springfield days, their lack of ego and ability to simply blend with him had afforded a sense of freedom and "the possibilities of doing more with my guitar and voice and feeling than anybody else". Crazy Horse gave him a monolithic rhythm and groove which he could attack with great chunks and jagged squalls of guitar. "I haven't had that rhythm for a while," Young had said, "and that's why I haven't been playing my guitar, because without that behind me I won't play. I mean, you can't get free enough."

Billy Talbot: "When Danny passed on, we didn't think of it happening again, Ralph or I. After we did *Tonight's The Night* with Neil, I ran into Poncho [Frank "Poncho" Sampedro] and *he* made me think we could do it again. We went down to Mexico and bought some cheap Spanish guitars and we were in a hotel room jamming, and in that jamming was this freedom and innocence. Our agenda was we just wanted to play music and feel good about it, and Poncho's attitude was just that. He didn't have some big ideas about what he was doing like, 'I'm a musician and I only play this and you're doing that' – because we had been playing with some guys, and they were cool guys and everything, but everybody had sort of their own agenda. And I thought, if we could bring that in – we weren't replacing Danny Whitten, because Danny was a different person completely, but it was something that I felt at the time just might happen – you know, give it a shot, it was fun, maybe we'll all have fun together. And, thank God, it worked out."

Talbot met Sampedro at a party. He had been in bands in Detroit since he was 11 years old, moving west when he was 17 to "become a star" as there was no place for rock stars then in Motown-dominated Motor City. He'd played here and there in Los Angeles, but nothing to write home about until Talbot introduced him to an equally enthusiastic Ralph Molina; they called up Young and invited him over to jam. At first Poncho was "timid" with Neil, but soon lost his nervousness. By the end of the day they had been recruited for his next album.

It was not, Young was careful to point out, a case of recapturing the chemistry they'd had with Whitten: "We just got a different chemistry. You can never get anything back. Danny's death changed the dynamics of the band but not the overall feeling of what we were about." The band concurred. "Danny's time with us was that time. He's still with us," explained Molina, "but in spirit," added Talbot. Poncho: "Yesterday's gone, we're here now – the main thing that happened was we were having fun."

Young had also talked in his interview about a new record he was thinking of calling 'Ride My Llama' (its songs about Aztecs and Incas and time-travel looked to be influenced by a poem called The Bridge about real and mythical pasts, written by the US poet Hart Crane). It wound up being named after the beach where he lived and recorded the album – at the house of friend and producer David Briggs, once again living nearby. Word was out that *Zuma* would mark a shift from the emotional wastelands of Young's last three albums, possibly even be another *Harvest*. Although certainly more accessible than anything since *Harvest*, it was a much harder, more electric record – Cortez The Killer was an almost Cowgirl In The Sand-type guitar epic, and Danger Bird featured what Lou Reed once said was the best guitar playing he had ever heard.

Legend has it that during its recording, Bob Dylan – himself newly single – was lurking in Briggs' driveway checking out what was going on, until they invited him inside. Dylan and Young had played together that March at a benefit concert (its high-profile cast, which included The Grateful Dead, The Miracles, The Doobie Brothers, Jefferson Starship, Santana and actor Marlon Brando, seeming somewhat top heavy for its aim of raising money and awareness for extra-curricular school sports). There was definitely a mutual appreciation society; Young loved *Blood On The Tracks*, which appeared the same year as *Zuma*, and was so taken with the idea behind Dylan's Rolling Thunder Revue – showing how "a major performer can live with his people" – that he borrowed it for himself.

After a successful operation to remove a node from his throat (the problem had got so bad he had taken to answering the phone by whistling), Young and Crazy Horse embarked on what soon became dubbed Rolling Zuma, a winter tour of tiny California bars. It was as spontaneous as a tour could be and had relatively no publicity – Young would call up a bar and volunteer their services for the night for free. Afterwards he would hang out for a beer and a chat with the fans. Anyone thinking these free, friendly performances manifested a '60s hippie ethic would have been quickly disillusioned by reports that, shortly beforehand, Young – the Woodstock graduate-turned-NIMBY – had successfully persuaded his local planning committee to veto an outdoor festival near his home. The bar shows were his ideal situation: intimacy with his audience, but in small numbers. And on his terms.

10 Eat A Peach

THE GARGANTUAN 1974 CSN&Y TOUR, ELLIOT
Roberts had said, "left a bad taste in the band's mouth". But
if a new album had failed to come out of it, the lines of
communication were still open. On *Zuma*'s closing track,
Through My Sails, Young had been joined by Crosby,
Stills and Nash; and when Stephen Stills's solo tour
brought him to Neil's neck of the woods, Young joined
him to play guitar (would have sung too if it wasn't for the
bad throat). A second get-together the same year led to
talk of emulating Crosby and Nash and making a Stills-
Young album. In January 1976, just after completing the
Rolling Zuma tour and before setting off with Crazy

Horse for Europe and Japan, the two got together at a Miami studio.

Though *Long May You Run* was launched in a mood of co-operation and camaraderie – perhaps augmented by the fact that their old Buffalo Springfield colleague Dewey Martin was suing them for the $150,000 in royalties that he claimed they duped him into signing away – Stills and Young had not written a single thing together. Young brought in five songs, Stills managed four, later griping that Young had made his contributions up on the spot and held anything special back for his own record. Certainly, apart from the title track – a love song to Mort, his 1948 Buick hearse – there was nothing here that compared with *Zuma*. And, since they were using Stills's backing band, it was easy to get the impression of Young just dropping by on his friend's album to lend a hand.

Sessions broke for three months for the Crazy Horse tour. Young, who brought a camera crew to Europe for his first shows since the controversial Tonight's The Night visit, captured everything on film – from waking up in bed in his hotel room, to the party at a London nightclub after the third of four Hammersmith Odeon shows, where Young in lumberjack shirt and earth shoes mingled with the likes of Kevin Ayers and Lynsey De Paul. "The longer I go," he told a Sounds journalist who cornered him, "the more I get trapped in my past." Sometimes, though, he set the traps himself: before resuming work with Stills back in America, he telephoned Crosby and Nash with the plan of making it a full CSN&Y reunion.

Once again, as it so often did, it started well and fell apart with a thud. When Crosby and Nash took a break to complete their duo album, Young and Stills wiped their vocals from the tapes and went back to working as a pair. Maybe it was a buddy bonding thing; maybe they were on a roll and wanted to get on with it; at one point Young was quoted as saying he didn't think CSN&Y's hippie half were "hungry enough" to do it properly. Whatever, Crosby and Nash were furious – though in the end they had the last laugh, their album *Whistling Down The Wire* doing better than the Stills-Young effort.

Long May You Run turned out to be an ironic title. A three-month tour set up in the summer of America's Bicentennial year lasted just 18 days before Young had enough. He turned his bus around on the way to a gig and headed for home, stopping off to send Stills a telegram. It read: "Dear Stephen, funny how some things that start spontaneously end that way. Eat a peach, Neil" (Allman Brothers fans will recognise the subtext of that last statement). The official statement from Young's camp a little more diplomatically blamed a recurrence of Young's throat problems. What Young said when he left The Buffalo Springfield was probably nearer to the truth: "I was going crazy. I needed more space."

"The funniest thing about the Stills-Young tour," said band member Joe Vitale, "was that we rehearsed for three weeks and the tour only lasted two – so we played a lot more up at his ranch than we did on the road. We had big crowds and great shows – it was a hell of a band, Neil and Stephen, George Perry on bass, Joe Lala on percussion, Jerry Aiello on keyboards, me on drums. We did Springfield songs, we did CSN&Y songs, we did Stephen songs and we did Neil songs. The one I remember doing that was so different from the original record was The Loner – it was just full-blown, kick-ass rock'n'roll. Stephen had come up with this new guitar riff and Neil immediately adhered to it and it was killer. The vibe between Neil and Stephen was really good – which was why I was so puzzled about Neil's leaving. I would have understood it a little better if Stephen and Neil had had some major blow-out, but they'd been having such a good time."

Rock critics weren't much impressed by the tour or the album, tending to see the latter as two cobbled-together solo EPs. "Young's work on the album leaves him right open to all the attacks made by the 'Poor Neil, dead as a doornail' school subsequent to *After The Gold Rush* and prior to *On The Beach*, which means that he's pissing in the wind and using his whine voice," wrote NME. A review of the live show in Sounds described a "heavily made-up" Stills ("maybe he's going on a talk show afterward") and a "dazed hippie" Young (with the complexion of "the underside of a sand-shark") taking it in turns to do individual greatest hits sets and leaving every 10 minutes for costume changes like a Cher show. By the end Young was sweating and Stills "still had all his hair in place". In the Battle Of The Guitarists the press turned the shows into Young definitely scored the higher points, even if he claimed that he wasn't trying to. "The one thing that everyone has always assumed is that there's a fundamental competition between us; in fact it's the difference between us that makes it work," he told Rolling Stone. "We're like brothers, you know. We love each other and we hate each other. We resent each other, but we love playing together." For a while.

While Young went back to Crazy Horse, Stills set about mending bridges with Crosby and Nash – successfully. Before long the three were in a Florida studio working on an album. One day a security guard noticed a suspicious-looking character in the bushes outside. It was Neil, who had dropped by to say hello and was taking a piss first. Remarkably grudge-free, the four made up. And, saying nothing about peaches, Stills and Young spent the Thanksgiving of '76 together, playing at The Band's farewell concert. The Martin Scorsese-directed documentary of the show, The Last Waltz, showed a happy-looking Young performing with a wodge of cocaine up his nose.

"Cocaine was a big, big deal at the time," said The Band's Levon Helm in his autobiography, This Wheel's On Fire. "[Promoter] Bill Graham had painted one of the dressing rooms white, walls and ceiling, and put a thick white rug on the floor. The only thing in the room was a sleek glass table with razor blades artfully strewn about." There was even a tape machine playing non-stop sniffing sounds. "Neil had delivered a good version of Helpless ... with a good-size rock of cocaine stuck in his nostril. Neil's manager said *no way* is Neil gonna be in the film like this. They had to go to special effects people who developed what they called a 'travelling booger matte' that sanitised Neil's nostril and put Helpless into the movie."

Young was also indulging in another rock-star pursuit – accumulating cars. Like his beloved Mort, they were all antiques, including a 1940s Cadillac with a bullet-proof window that once belonged to a Latin American dictator. He bought a boat (The Evening Coconut) too, and a big old schooner to restore. Indulging his bachelor-hood fantasies to the limit, Young moved into a house with a bunch of male friends in Santa Cruz – a small coastal town 30 miles south of his ranch – and joined their rock'n'roll bar band The Ducks; audiences were encouraged to quack at appropriate junctures. Jeff Blackburn, ex Moby Grape, who'd known Neil since The

Buffalo Springfield, told him they were looking for a guitar player and he applied for the job. Doing their own roadying in one of Young's car collection – a Packard station wagon dubbed, naturally, the Duckmobile – they played a couple of dozen local, low-key, unpublicised shows, democratically sharing the songwriting and the pay (on their best night taking home $180 apiece).

The Ducks quacked their last when word spread about what was going on. His anonymity gone and the Duckhouse burgled, Young took off for Florida in his bus. The double album's worth of material made with The Ducks remained unreleased, while Neil – making the most of his last few months as a single man – went to work on his boat.

11 Ploughin' Time Again

IN THE SPRING OF '77, YOUNG WAS BACK UP AT his ranch and working on a new record, *American Stars'N'Bars*. He had planned it as a two-part concept album, half about American social history, half about American bars. It wound up concentrating more on the second half – country and western songs full of booze-fuelled boisterousness, lust and tears. They required a female voice or two, so Young called old friend Linda Ronstadt, who showed up with a backing-singer friend of hers Nicolette Larson, whom Young had met at her house a couple of years before. He nicknamed them The Saddle Bags.

"He'd had this idea of a bar-band sound, using a couple of chick singers from some local bar," said Larson, "but I don't think it worked and he decided to go the other way using Linda Ronstadt and me."

Unlike his last album, *Long May You Run*, *American Stars'N'Bars* was made in an instant. The first side was recorded live – so live that Larson and Ronstadt thought they were just practising and didn't know the tape was running. Larson: "Neil doesn't like to do a lot of takes. He used to use the phrase 'ring of truth'. He'd say, 'If somebody wants to hear a perfect Neil Young record they can buy my first album' – which he hated."

"We recorded it all in a day at Neil's ranch," recalled Poncho, "everything except Like A Hurricane." The first appearance of the song that was a superb part of the live show, even if it did sound somewhat tamer here, took them a little longer. "We'd been trying to record it with two guitars, bass and drums and Neil was kind of giving up on it, and when he started walking out of the studio I played this string instrument" – Poncho is cred- ited on the sleeve as "Stringman" – "and he decided to pick up his guitar. We played it once and at the end of the take he said, 'I think that's the way it goes', and that's the one on the record." Also on the record was a handful of songs from sessions done in '75 and '76, including Home-grown, title track of the album Young had written about his break-up with Carrie Snodgress, rejected in favour of *Tonight's The Night*.

American Stars'N'Bars did not get great reviews. Though praised for his "use of strings" and "creatively-wielded extraneous noise" (Sounds), the words that came up more often were "schizophrenic", "uneven", "muddled", "annoying" and "lazy" – some of them, with the exception of "lazy", having some validity. When the album was released in June '77, Young already had another project on the go. He was compiling a triple-album retrospective, *Decade*. "I think it tells a story," he wrote in the sleevenotes. "This could be the record that defines my influence on the music world for the past 10 years." In a piece for Sounds headlined Hero, Legend Or Clod?, Tim Lott summed up what, for many fans, that influence had been: "He angers me bitterly . . . but displays flashes of such intense talent it near blurs your eyes. Not often enough, though. The man is a total inspiration. The man is a total idiot." Young just shrugged, as he always did. As he said some years later, "One week I'm a jerk, the next I'm a genius."

By autumn 1977, with *Decade* out and selling and his crew doing a good job fixing up his 100-foot Baltic trader named the W.N. Ragland, after his grandfather, Young was in Nashville with Nicolette Larson and his newly-assembled big ensemble, The Gone With The Wind Orchestra. They played just one show together at the Miami Music Festival. The set included an unreleased song called Lady Wingshot, said to be written to Larson. Young and his backing singer had become an item.

It was a short-lived romance; more a stepping-stone to his marriage to Pegi Morton. During the Christmas of '77, while Nicolette was staying at Broken Arrow, he dropped by to visit Pegi, a neighbour, with whom he had gone out some years earlier. Soon after, Nicolette was living in his house in Zuma and Pegi was living with Neil at the ranch, playing ma and pa to Zeke, who visited at weekends. Young had designated one of the barns for an elaborate model railroad, ostensibly for his son, and was on his hands and knees pouring concrete and constructing embankments and terrains. Staying at the ranch for the best part of half a year – in Neil Young terms positively Lennonesque in its house-husbandness – he immersed himself once again in the role of family man, before reappearing onstage at San Francisco's tiny Boarding House in May '78, with a "band" of wooden cigar-store Indians. His manager called the five-night fundraiser for the club where Captain Beefheart used to play, "the one-stop world tour".

Three months later Neil and Pegi were married. Since there was an upcoming tour with Crazy Horse to rehearse and yet another new album to finish, the honeymoon was delayed. With *Comes A Time* in the can, Neil and the pregnant Pegi set off for the Bahamas on board the Ragland; the film editor who had been working with him on Human Highway and his friend David Briggs and their respective wives came along too. While bobbing about on the turquoise waves, Young had an idea for shows involving giant props and strange costumes. When the boat docked in Florida, he had two weeks to get them designed and made in time for the tour.

The simple, accessible album *Comes A Time*,

recorded in Nashville with The Gone With The Wind Orchestra (including J.J. Cale, Crazy Horse, Ben Keith, Spooner Oldham and ex-girlfriend Nicolette Larson) was in stark contrast to the loud, theatrical tour. Said Larson, "It wound up being kind of a duet record . . . With Neil and me, singing together was just like Fred and Ginger." She would later have a big solo hit covering one of the album's songs, Lotta Love. "I got that song off a tape I found lying on the floor of Neil's car," she said. "I popped it in the tape player and commented on what a great song it was. Neil said, 'You want it? It's yours.'"

The British rock press was less impressed with his new material (NME: "*American Stars'N'Bars* was often bad, this is worse – it's often bland . . . As ordinary as Neil Young is ever likely to get"). Then, in late punk era Britain it was not likely to go down well. But in America, which was still quite immune from the New Wave explosion, it was his biggest hit since *Harvest*.

Comes A Time came from "a soft place", said Young on the Rust tour. "But I'm somewhere else now."

12 Rust, Honey And Carpet Fluff

SCURRYING ABOUT TO THE SOUND OF JIMI Hendrix's Star Spangled Banner, a hooded stage-crew dressed like the Star Wars Jawas with red flashlights for eyes readied the arena stage for the show: a 15-foot-tall microphone, an enormous sequinned amp, oversized equipment trunks 30 feet above the ground. Slowly the "road-eyes" tugged on the ropes that removed the lid from one of the cases to reveal Neil Young lying asleep, his acoustic guitar by his side. Rubbing his eyes, he stood up, looking small and vulnerable in his white playclothes and with his newly close-cropped hair. Opening with his most innocent songs, Sugar Mountain and I Am A Child, he clambered down and wandered about the stage, singing through a wireless mic. As the show went on the music got progressively louder, culminating in an electric wall of sound. The music was punctuated by coneheads and white-coated hospital doctors and avoid-the-bad-acid Woodstock loudspeaker announcements, as well as by the ever-busy road-eyes. Pegi was a road-eye. So was just about anyone who happened to be backstage and couldn't run fast enough. "We'd walk in and all these guys who'd been working with us, the truck drivers and everything, were all putting on black-face and getting their outfits on," said Poncho, "instead of going, 'Oh here comes the band, they've got it easy.' Which is a beautiful thing."

It was meant to be a tale of rock'n'roll innocence and its growth and corruption through experience; part serious, a bigger part fun. "The longer I keep going the more I have to fight this corrosion," Young said in an LA radio interview with Mary Turner. It was designed as a fun show, he said, because "I don't take it so seriously as before. When you look back at the old bands, they're just not that funny; people want to be funny now, people want to have a good time. That's why the punk thing is so good and healthy. People who make fun of the established rock scene, like Devo and The Ramones, are much more vital to my ears than what's been happening in the last four or five years. I like Donna Summer, though," he added. "I think she's pretty good."

Young had discovered punk on his 1976 European tour. Its intensity and energy appealed to him; even more attractive was his discovery that most of his peers hated it. Rock, in America especially, had become flaccid and middle-aged, complacent and corrupt. So when he got a call from his old friend Dean Stockwell raving about a weird and wonderful New Wave band called Devo that his wife Toni Basil had turned him onto and that he and Iggy Pop had just been to see at an LA club, Young was intrigued. After hearing their self-produced Mongoloid single and watching their short home-made film The Truth About De-Evolution, Young called Elliot Roberts, who immediately offered to be their manager.

"Neil was putting together Human Highway at the time and he knew that I directed Devo's videos and Mark [Mothersbaugh] and I came up with all the ideas," said Jerry Casale, "and he said, 'I have these places where you can be in the movie. What would you like to do?' He was making it up as he went along. Dean Stockwell and Dennis Hopper were making up parts of it with him. Frankly, we thought, with our methodology and our sensibility, that what we were watching was some kind of indulgent hippie project. Everybody on the set was loaded; Dennis Hopper – he'd just become a Hollywood screw-up at that point – was chasing Sally Kirkland around with a big knife, basically being [Blue Velvet's] Frank Booth in real life."

Young suggested that his flummoxed new collaborators write a scene starring themselves as nuclear waste workers. "We came up with a scenario where we were bitching about our jobs at the nuclear plant and then we'd break into song like in an old musical – this twisted version of an old folk song by The Kingston Trio, It Takes A Worried Man; of course, what *we* were worried about was modern things like the end of the planet." There was a "groovy granola mentality", he said, in the cheap, funky east Hollywood studio where they recorded the song, with Young in his Sex Pistols T-shirt and various of his friends hanging out. "He acts completely low-key, soft-spoken, anti-intellectual, no idea what's going on – if you didn't know who he was, you might think he was a kind of a moron. Like the character he played in Human Highway, only he did it every day. Convincingly."

Adding to the sense of surreality for Casale and Mothersbaugh was that they'd been art students at Kent State University at the time of the riots that had inspired Ohio. "We couldn't believe we were working with the guy who had written Ohio, a song that directly related to something we were in the middle of, running from the National Guard throwing teargas at us. I knew two of the four people who were killed very well and I was maybe 50 yards from Alison Krauss when she was shot in the back. But we thought of Neil Young in terms of a certain era and mentality. Though when you think about it, he's really kind of a Devo character himself. Although his music was totally different, his personal iconoclasm and scepticism about the world and organised authority was just the same as ours."

To raise the money to make Devo's singles, Casale and Mothersbaugh used to have a small T-shirt design and printing business; one day Mark was wearing one of their efforts that sported the slogan "Rust Never Sleeps". "It meant the enemy that never goes away," said Casale. "We did it for a rust-removal company. Neil just flipped out. He used it for the title of his album."

Rust Never Sleeps was half acoustic, half electric, its songs raging from the beautifully poignant to the downright menacing. Thrasher reflected his feelings towards the bloated, mid-'70s "dead weight" CSN&Y. Powderfinger was a song he'd sent Ronnie Van Zant two years before to use on his next Lynyrd Skynyrd album, but thanks to a fatal plane crash he never did. My My, Hey Hey, which name-checked Johnny Rotten and was reprised in an electric version Hey Hey, My My, was "probably the most bitter, ironic and honest statement about rock'n'roll and its attendant lifestyle," wrote Nick Kent in NME, hailing *Rust Never Sleeps* as "the finest album Neil Young has ever released". Sounds called it "the best Sex Pistols record since Pretty Vacant".

A second Rust album followed five months later – *Live Rust*, recorded on the tour. Both albums made the charts, surprisingly perhaps doing better in America than in Britain (8 and 15 in the US as against 13 and 55 in the

UK). "Both *Rust*s," said Sounds, "are just about the best dirty, noisy, sloppy and downright crazed albums since the MC5 went clean on *Back In The USA*. The guitar always sounds like Young's dipped the strings in a mixture of honey and carpet fluff before coming on-stage."

Even Bernard Shakey finally came in for some good press. Five years after the slated Journey Through The Past, Young's director *alter ego* found success and critical acclaim with his Rust Never Sleeps concert movie, generally acknowledged as one of the best ever made. Sadly it did not help him get backing for Human Highway.

WHO WAS THAT MASKED MAN? – THE LOST YEARS

13 Communication Breakdown

It's good to have different identities in life, par-
ticularly if you're me, because I wake up in the
morning and don't know who I am anyway. It often
takes quite a while to work out who I am.

THE '80S. THOUGH SOME MAY RECALL THEM
with warmth, for those of us of a certain age and sensibility they were the Anti-'60s. Yuppies instead of Yippies;
Thatcher, Reagan, city traders, power haircuts. The
decade of selfishness-as-virtue – hiding in the bathroom
with your Walkman on and chopping yourself a line
instead of sharing a joint with friends, hoping to Krishna

no-one drops a hot bit on your new vinyl LP. Vinyl – that's another thing, soon to be obsolete as a hugely expanding music industry geared up to make us buy our record collection all over again on shiny, new, digitally-improved, but infinitely less loveable CDs. The decade, too, of style-as-necessity, as MTV, launched in '81, overnight made music's look as important as its sound.

Young, for a maverick, turned out to be very much a man of the '80s. Severing himself as good as totally from the counter-culture he had only partially subscribed to in the first place, he spent much of the decade blithely hopping from style to style. Electro-pop, rockabilly, good ol' boy country, turgid synth-rock, R&B – a series of exasperating albums, some so wilfully capricious that they seemed like a put-on. Either that or a rock star's male menopause – the new toys required for keeping the musical pecker up.

Of course, Neil Young being Neil Young, the truth was far more complex. The constant changing, always a trademark, was as much a psychological necessity as a musical statement. The "Me" he presented in the Me Decade was a deliberately confusing one – a means of preventing people *knowing* him, letting them get too close. At the risk of cod-Freudianism I'd venture this went back to his childhood: his parents' divorce, separation from his brother, and the childhood polio that found him masked and quarantined in a big-city hospital. By 1980, Young was pretty damn desperate for any mask he could get.

The '70s had ended for Young, just as they had begun, on a musical high note. The Village Voice voted him Artist of the Decade. With the remarkable body of work he had produced, and so much of it essential, in the minds of many he was now *the* American artist. And as the decade unfolded – John Lennon murdered at the end of 1980; Dylan embracing a religion that appeared to require recording crap LPs – his position seemed unassailable. "When the '80s come," Dylan had said, "we've got to have all our cards on the table or we'll be out of the game." Trouble was, Young had been dealt a hell of a hand.

The son that Pegi gave birth to in November '78 was failing to develop normally. The following year doctors diagnosed cerebral palsy – the same disorder his half-brother Zeke had suffered from, but of a far more serious nature. Ben could neither walk nor talk. Young was devastated. Helpless, wracked with guilt that he was responsible – "I couldn't believe it. There were two different mothers. It couldn't have happened twice" – the doctors assured him it was an ugly coincidence, something over which he had no control. Not an easy concept for a man like Young to get his brain around. Pegi, meanwhile, had other things on her mind, literally. Rushed into hospital in March 1980 for an operation on a brain tumour, she'd been given a 50/50 chance of coming out alive. Young made up his mind there and then that he was "going to take care of Pegi, take care of the kids. I shut the door on my music." It was quite a shift. In the past his music had always come first; everyone and everything else tied for second place. "I always thought that my music was more important than anything else," he told his father, "but now I know that music is important only in that it reflects where I'm at."

That his first album of the '80s, *Hawks & Doves*, was a shadow of its brilliant predecessor was understandable. Though its content gave little indication of the personal turbulence Young was going through, with the benefit of hindsight the marital commitment expressed in Staying

Power and the almost right-wing lyrical stance elsewhere make sense: being shut away at the ranch, fighting for his wife and kids, had a quasi-survivalist connotation that gelled with the brash individualism, family values and militarism of the Reagan years.

During '80 and '81, Young rarely left Broken Arrow to play; he and Pegi, now recovered, had signed up with the Institute For The Achievement Of Human Potential to a rigorous programme for Ben which required spending 12 hours a day, every day, on tough mental and physical exercises. Life centred around the child. The house was adapted for the stimulation equipment "The Program" called for. It was, he said, "the most difficult thing I've ever done". Ben was crying all the time. The exercises were endlessly repetitive. How he found time to get any work done at all is a wonder. Since the short bursts of free time were more conducive to film work – and the celluloid world preferable to the one he was in – he wrote music for the Hunter Thompson movie Where The Buffalo Roam and continued work on his own film, Human Highway.

"A comedy about a tragedy," his second collaboration with Dean Stockwell was an offbeat story about ecological disaster. Young had the role of Lionel Switch, a dim motor mechanic with fantasies of being a rock star. He had another role, too – as writer/director "Bernard Shakey". Right now Young relished role-playing more than ever. Masking what was really going on inside was not just a way of messing with the fans' and music industry's attempts to contain and define him – his '80s genre-hopping was, after all, a pretty effective way of telling them, "You think you know me? Try this!" – it was also an essential self-preservation device, just as moody "Neil the Indian" had hidden the insecure epileptic in The Buffalo Springfield, and the sports-coated motor-mouth on the Tonight's The Night tour had concealed the man tormented by his friends' deaths.

Then again, maybe he just had a low boredom threshold . . .

At the end of 1980 Young summoned Crazy Horse to the ranch to record *Re-ac-tor*. "Neil was spending a lot of time with his son, so we didn't spend quite the time on that album that maybe we should have," said Frank Sampedro. "We just kind of put it together. His mind wasn't focused on the music a lot then, he had other things on his mind. It really shows, I think."

Re-ac-tor reflected Young's life perfectly, from the title – its fragmentation at once encompassing his current obsessions with nuclear energy, being an actor, and his and his wife and son's fractured lives – to the tough, angry, repetitive music. The guitar playing was claustrophobic. Lyrics once again took an America-is-best position – odd from someone who had held so firmly onto Canadian citizenship. On a different tack, one of the album's finest moments, Southern Pacific, manifested his longtime love of trains. The six-year-old who had clutched his toy train to his chest in the back of the car speeding him off to the polio ward had completed the "train barn" (ostensibly for Ben) at the ranch: 4,000 square feet of state-of-the-art, remote-controlled model railway, most of its features constructed by Young himself. A decade later Young would go further and purchase the old American model railway company, Lionel Trains.

Interestingly, Young would later refer to his genre albums as being "like little movies. It's a character thing. Maybe if someone had asked me to make a movie I would have done that instead of making a record." Following Human Highway's premiere in January '82 it was highly unlikely anyone would ask him to make another movie. "One of the worst films anyone, anywhere, has ever made," wrote Vox, as it went straight to video. "A plotless ramble through really duff comedy." The film, like his music, was full of ideas; unlike his music, though, he still seemed unable to fashion them into something affecting.

By the summer, though, things at home were looking up enough for Young to leave on tour – shows a short distance from the ranch first, then a longer European Transband jaunt. Neil and Pegi had switched Ben from the "Nazi" "Program" to a less all-consuming one under the auspices of the National Academy For Child Development (who would name them their Parents of the Year), which concentrated on developing communication skills. Engrossed by finding ways for the non-oral child to communicate, Young acquired a vocoder. He used it on *Trans*, singing like a robot dog over a Kraftwerkian techno-disco beat.

Trans, he said later, was "an incredibly personal

record, maybe the most personal thing I've done". But since at the time he failed to make its motivation public, insisting only "I've always loved machines" and "if you don't experiment you're dead", *Trans*, like father and son, failed to communicate.

14 The Starmaker Machinery Behind The Popular Song

BETWEEN *RE-AC-TOR* AND *TRANS*, YOUNG HAD switched record companies. After 13 years with Reprise – Frank Sinatra's label, taken over by Warners when the singer was diverted by his Vegas casino business – the relationship was beginning to sour (Surfer Joe And Moe The Sleaze on *Re-ac-tor* is thought to have been a dig at Reprise boss Mo Ostin and his sidekick). Young was looking elsewhere at the same time that David Geffen – Young's manager Elliot Roberts's former partner – was seeking a status star to boost his eponymous record label's fading fortunes now that John Lennon, after just one

Geffen album, was dead. RCA had come up with a much larger offer to sign Young, but Geffen, Roberts told his UK fan club magazine Broken Arrow in '82, "has no preconceived notions about Neil . . . I think that at the end of five years we will see that Neil's record sales will more than make up for the money we refused to take now, because he will have the freedom to practise his art as he sees it, as opposed to when you make a deal where someone is paying you £1–2 million an album you feel obligated to give them commercial music that they can sell large numbers of. Neil's not concerned with selling large numbers of his records, he's concerned with making records that he's pleased with. David Geffen relates to that. He knows Neil may do a country album and then he may do an electric album because there's no rhyme or reason with Neil. It's what he's moved by."

This was not quite the case when Young offered his new label their first album, *Island In The Sun*. Geffen didn't want it. Since his last two Reprise albums hadn't done so well critically or commercially, Geffen evidently wanted to start the relationship with a surefire success. Its replacement, *Trans*, scraped into the UK Top 20 – helped by the European tour, outwardly a gesture to the fans he'd ignored on the Rust tour but probably as much an attempt to find an audience more sympathetic to experimental music than his adopted countrymen. Back home, though, it lagged behind. For the US tour, Young dropped his Transband – various Stray Gators, Santa Monica Flyers, Ducks and Buffalo Springfield stalwarts reshuffled – and toured alone with a computer, duetting with his image on the backdrop screen. Towards the end of the tour, on-stage in Kentucky, he collapsed. The resident doctor, who doubled as the county coroner – a fact not likely to inspire confidence – found Young still breathing and prescribed the US equivalent of Lucozade for low blood-sugar, plus Halcyon (the now-outlawed sleeping pill once favoured by Bryan Ferry) for his exhaustion. Neither worked too well. It was weeks before Young was up and about, and when he was he went to Nashville to work on a new record with the *Harvest* and *Comes A Time* musicians, *Old Ways*.

A return to his popular country-rock style? Sounds like a surefire success to us. But once again Geffen rejected it. It was "too country"; rock was what was selling in the early '80s. So Neil gave them rock – old-time rock-abilly rock. *Everybody's Rockin'* had the double attraction of being music that Young personally loved, which he could record on Geffen's dollar while simultaneously giving him the finger. (Later, he would consider the album "as good as *Tonight's The Night*", blaming Geffen for cancelling a couple of sessions before he'd finished it and "given (it) a lot more depth".)

The album appeared the same month that David Crosby was nodding off in court as the judge sentenced him to five years in prison on charges of possessing drugs and a concealed gun. His insouciant old colleague, meanwhile, was out on the road as Neil Young And The Shocking Pinks, dressed in a pink and black '50s suit, his hair Brylcreemed back, accompanied by dancing girls The Pinkettes, his wife Pegi among them.

"Neil was having the best time in the world," said Craig Hayes, aka Shocking Pinks sax player and MC Vito Toledo. "He had his wife and youngest son with him and his daughter Amber was conceived on that tour."

Geffen did not share his enthusiasm. In November '83 the record company boss sued his former management client for $3 million in damages for making albums "which were not commercial in nature and musically uncharacteristic of Young's previous records". Quite which previous records was not made entirely clear. Young, as you do, counter-sued, demanding $21 million for fraud and breach of contract. All the talk about respect for artistic integrity and musician-friendly environment had evaporated.

Although it was no doubt upsetting being taken to court by a large, rich corporation, especially one with the delicate task of handling your artistic output, at the same time it must have been gratifying to have such public validation of what you'd been saying you wanted from your career all along: to be characteristically uncharacteristic. But new developments at home made it an anxious time for Neil. Pegi was pregnant again. To take his mind off what might happen, he went back out on tour, gathering Crazy Horse around him for protection like drone bees. They stopped off in New York to make an album, but nothing sounded right. Bringing in session guys only made things worse. It was abandoned and replaced with a second version of *Old Ways* he'd recorded with The

International Harvesters. If Geffen thought the original was too country, this one was gather round the hearth under the Home Sweet Home sampler and listen to Grand Ole Opry. "It's hard to teach a dinosaur a new trick," the title track's lyrics goaded his label boss.

June '84, a month after Pegi gave birth to a perfectly healthy baby girl Amber Jean, Young, dressed like a farmhand, old checked shirt and ponytail, went off on the road with his country band – pedal steel, fiddle, banjo – and support acts Waylon Jennings and Jessie Colter, Johnny Paycheck and The Judds. Stretching out over a year, the tour took in family-friendly outdoor events like state fairs, usually the provenance of mainstream C&W. Soon to turn 40, Young said he was getting too old for electric rock. Country musicians, however, were out there playing and making records way past the rock artist's sell-by date. They also promoted traditional down-home, all-American family values: "In country music I see people who take care of their own," he told The Guardian. "You've got 75-year-old guys on the road. That's what I was put here to do, so I want to make sure that I surround myself with people who are going to take care of me because I'm in it for the long run."

Not that Young was ever much of a revolutionary, but the things he was coming out with in interviews – taking care of one's own, ensuring a strong America ("It was wrong to have let the armed forces deteriorate"), blanket praise for the land of the free ("I'm tired of listening to people say that America is bad everywhere, that we're a bunch of aggressive animals and don't have any cool") – were light-years away from '60s liberalism. For his older fans, his pro-Reagan speech at his New Orleans show was up there with Bowie's Nazi salute. And his "we were just trying to help" spin on Vietnam – the war that had united his generation and fuelled the counter-culture – was the final nail in the coffin.

As to how much of it was over-enthusiasm for the role he'd adopted and how much raging conservatism is hard to judge. Certainly, as a ploy to get his new record label off his back, it was as Machiavellian and effective as anything David Geffen could have come up with. Geffen, knowing when he was beat, dropped his lawsuit in '85 after Young informed him that henceforth he would play nothing but country music so that by the time the case came to court it would cease to be "unrepresentative".

Later, his wounds somewhat soothed by the success his record company was enjoying with heavy rockers Aerosmith and Guns N' Roses, the businessman immortalised in Joni Mitchell's Free Man In Paris would claim, "The truth is I fought with him because I wanted him to do better work. Because I love him." But by the time *Old Ways* Mark II appeared in the summer of '85, truth was getting to be a nebulous concept, as the line between consummate role-player and wealthy rock star worn down by responsibility became increasingly blurred.

15 Feed The Farmers

THE CHILDREN OF THE '60s, FOR ALL THEIR talk, didn't really go in all that much for free shows (Woodstock, remember, was an accident) or charity concerts; the drugs of choice, pot and acid, do tend to dull the organisational skills. But after Christmas '84 and Band Aid's Do They Know It's Christmas? single, a sudden wind of compassion blew across the Atlantic and through the air-conditioning systems of palatial pop-star homes. Americans gathered together to make their own "feed the world"-type song, while Young joined fellow-Canadians Joni Mitchell, Ronnie Hawkins, Gordon Lightfoot and, er, Anne Murray on Bryan Adams's fund-raiser Tears Are Not

Enough. Although he was accused of singing flat during the recording, no-one said a word about the incongruity of openly backing Reagan and his war machine while weeping for a Third World country ravaged by famine and conflict. Young also agreed to reunite with CSN&Y for Live Aid, Crosby having been released on appeal. First, though, he played at Willie Nelson's Fourth of July picnic alongside country stars Johnny Cash, Kris Kristofferson, Waylon Jennings, Jerry Jeff Walker, David Allen Coe and, of course, Willie Nelson, with whom Young duetted on his single Are There Any More Real Cowboys?

And so to Live Aid – "the biggest pop event staged over a one-day period", as "St Bob" Geldof described it, held simultaneously over a 16-hour period on July 15 at London's Wembley and Philadelphia's JFK stadiums. Young performed with the International Harvesters. Billy Talbot: "When he was doing Live Aid I was working at some job and I was *real* pissed off, because we weren't up there doing Hurricane and songs like that for billions of people all over the world instead of the country stuff. But that's in the past . . ."

The US show's headliner Bob Dylan, seemingly

infected by the same '80s outbreak of Reaganite patriotism as Young, muttered on-stage during his performance that they could do with taking a couple of million of the dollars raised from the concert to help their own farmers, who were suffering under the weight of crippling mortgages. It was more likely another example of Americans not quite believing that anywhere else really exists than Bob equating pestilence with bankruptcy. But something struck a chord. Dylan discussed what he'd said with Young after the show, who discussed it with Willie Nelson, who earlier that year had discussed something similar with Ray Charles during the recording of USA For Africa's We Are The World, and would now discuss it with the Governor of Illinois, one of his golfing pals, who promised to get them a stadium. Nelson and John Mellencamp divided up the task of recruiting country and pop performers; Young took the Geldofian role of meeting with farmers' groups to find out what they needed and relaying the information to the politicians in Washington DC, and within three months Farm Aid was born. Joining Young and the aforementioned in raising $10 million for the cause were Joni Mitchell, Lou Reed,

Tom Petty, B.B. King, Billy Joel, Loretta Lynn and Young's childhood hero Roy Orbison.

Over the next year Young played at benefits across the ideological spectrum, from Greenpeace and environmental charity Get Tough On Toxics to Vietnam Veterans and Farm Aid II. Closer to home, he set up the Bridge School – which Pegi would run – for disabled and non-oral children. Its 1986 fund-raising concert would become, like Farm Aid, an annual star-studded event. He said that having two disabled children had made him feel "that God was trying to show me something, so I try to do as much as I can for handicapped kids and their families. I have a lot of compassion for those people and a lot of understanding that I didn't have before, and I think it's made me a better person."

After inducting the Everly Brothers into the brand-new Rock and Roll Hall of Fame, he got to work on a follow-up to *Old Ways*. Not country this time but the dense synth-rock *Landing On Water*. The band he chose to take it on the road emphasised the rock over the synth – Crazy Horse. Lasting most of the second half of '86 and the first half of '87, Young's longest tour since 1973 and his most extensive with Crazy Horse since *Rust* was once again theatrical. The curtain, painted to look like a garage door, rose to reveal the band "practising" in a clutter of garden tools, tyres and abandoned appliances, while film was projected on the window behind them and mechanical spiders and cockroaches crawled about. Neil's "mum", hanging out clothes at the start of the show, would reappear to warn them that the exterminators were on their way, and white-coated men in gas masks would spray the stage with dry ice. The critics loved it.

But when "The Third Best Garage Band In The World", as they billed themselves, arrived in Europe in the spring of '87 for their first tour in five years – propless, the stage set apparently too expensive to transport – tickets weren't exactly flying out the door, with the memory of the *Trans* tour still fresh in some minds. Outside Britain some shows had been cancelled. Relations between Neil and Crazy Horse were strained; Young, planning a documentary movie (the unreleased Muddy Track), captured it all on the camcorder he nicknamed "Otto" and trained almost constantly on everyone. When they returned to the States – with a quick diversion to Winnipeg for Neil to reunite with his high-school band The Squires – Young and Crazy Horse recorded the fifth and (thankfully) last of his Geffen albums, *Life*, a record that tied with *Journey Through The Past* as the recipient of his worst-ever album reviews.

"Some tracks we did in the studio, some tracks we took from live shows," said Frank Sampedro of the album, which was at least better than its predecessor, "and literally stripped them down and used the basic track again and rebuilt. Other things we just took from live shows and took the audience out, because we played so well. We find that we work better live . . . We're not *per se* studio musicians who can just play perfect tracks over and over again, we're more of an emotional-feeling, passionate-type band."

Which was one of the reasons Young had always given for wanting to go and work with CSN&Y – that Crazy Horse weren't musically sophisticated enough to handle some of the material he wrote. Another reason for reuniting with CSN&Y during a break in the Rusted-Out Garage tour for a brace of Greenpeace shows was moral obligation. He'd announced earlier in a radio interview that he would have another go at following up 1970's *Déjà Vu* if David Crosby – the man addressed in *Landing On Water*'s jaundiced Hippie Dream – got over his cocaine habit. When he said it, he doubtless thought it a pigs-might-fly situation but, wouldn't you know it, the porker was now out of jail and rehab and fully airborne. And so, undeterred by fears that Geffen would put a stop to his stubbornly uncommercial artist making a bound-to-be-successful CSN&Y album, or by rumours that Stephen Stills had taken over where Crosby left off in the drugs department, the four went into the studio.

This time things went well. Unfortunately, it co-incided with Young's realisation of how very much he wanted to play with his new R&B outfit. The Bluenotes – initially Crazy Horse plus horn section, though a second incarnation, swapping Ralph Molina and Billy Talbot for Chad Cromwell and Rich Rosas, recorded the album – gave him another new role to play: Blues Brother-cum-wino frontman, Shaky Deal (a self-mocking reference maybe, like Bernard Shakey, to his history of health problems). Their sound, as evidenced on *This Note's For You*, his first album back with Warner-Reprise, was boisterous and exuberant. (After Geffen, his old label must have seemed the model of tolerance and accommodation.) Young dubbed it "The Dawn Of Power-Swing". An offer to Reprise founder Frank Sinatra to guest on it did not meet with the desired response, but critics gave it the kindest reviews of Young's "genre" albums. And the anti-corporate-sponsorship song, This Note's For You, a take-off of beer ad jingle This Bud's For You, gave him a minor hit single. More valuably, when MTV banned its Julien Temple-directed video – its celebrity spoofs, like Michael Jackson's hair-igniting Pepsi ad, upset the advertisers – it gave him an opportunity for righteous indignation and upped his maverick status. MTV not only backed down but gave it their Video Of The Year Award, which Young was happy to accept ("Why be an enemy of MTV? It's bad enough never getting played on the radio."). But then he seemed happy all round with The Bluenotes (their name changed to Ten Men Working after Harold Melvin's successful court injunction), if only because "no-one was shouting for Southern Man like they've done throughout my whole fucking career". There was talk of making a live album, *This Note's For You Too*. But in another of his musical

U-turns – as Frank Sampedro put it, "Neil never turns corners, he ricochets around them" – he opted instead for an album of heavy electric feedback music.

Soon after the second CSN&Y studio album, *American Dream*, finally appeared, Young and his latest band The Restless (named after well-known US soap opera The Young And The Restless and renamed The Lost Dogs after Young's hound Elvis went missing) made the "abrasive" limited-edition EP, *Eldorado* (just 5,000 copies, released only in Australia and Japan). An album in the same vein was abandoned as he turned his attention towards the more diverse *Freedom*. The reasons he gave in a Radio One interview showed the kind of business awareness Young had deliberately distanced himself from during the rest of the 1980s: "I thought *Eldorado* by itself was a really fine album but, you know, if you don't have a record they can play on the radio you might as well forget it. You might as well not put out a record. So I took the songs that really created the feeling of *Eldorado* and put them out as an EP. At least I didn't have to put myself through this exasperating experience of trying to get something I felt was really me on the radio only to find out over and over again that no-one's gonna play it because it doesn't fit with some format. I'm sick of that." People could relate the songs on *Freedom*, he said, "to whatever it is they liked about me 15 years ago".

Following the *Rust Never Sleeps* blueprint, *Freedom*'s half-acoustic, half-electric tracks were sandwiched between two versions of one song: the anthem Rockin' In The Free World. The flag-waving, commie-bashing free world manifested earlier had been substituted with a decaying country riddled with problems – drugs, homelessness, crime, desperation. "Neil Young sounds as if he's teetering between protest, despair and acceptance," said an admiring Q. Rolling Stone made it Album Of The Year. It was Young's most critically acclaimed album of the decade.

The '80s ended for Neil – as had the '60s and '70s – on a musical high note. He'd surfed the sewage of bloated stadium superstardom, dabbled in no end of shit, but had still come out smelling like a rose. Somehow, through all the problems of the '80s – a pretty dire decade in itself, without the addition of disabled children, sick wife and your own record company disliking your art enough to sue – Young had kept the faith.

Years later, when looking back on his '80s output, Young would take one of three tacks: confrontational ("I really like it"; "Fuck them, I don't need them to tell me if I'm OK or not"; "My whole career is based on systematic destruction"), contextual ("What happened was that I just wasn't being accessible. Maybe my '80s music should just be looked at as one record. Maybe it would be easier for people to understand") or confessional ("I was deadly serious about what I was doing because I desperately needed to do something, but at the same time I didn't want my innermost feelings about life and everything to come out").

As he told the Village Voice, "I closed myself down so much [to the hurt] that I was doing great with surviving – but my soul was completely encased. I didn't even consider that I would need a soul to play my music, that when I shut the door on pain I shut the door on my music. It was what I did." He added, "and that's how people grow old."

Young's pet-name for CSN&Y's *American Dream*, incidentally, was *Geriatrics' Revenge.*

THE GODFATHER

16 Plugged

The truth is I was a lot older 10 or 15 years ago than I am now.

GRIZZLED AND WEATHER-BEATEN, HIS STOOP more pronounced than ever, weighed down by sideburns the shape and size of Madagascar, Neil Young still managed to charge into the '90s, body, soul and credibility pretty much intact.

"I'm like an old car," he told The Times. "When I came out I was a very cool car, then I got a bit used and there were all these other newer models, and pretty soon it was time to put me in the junkyard and use me for parts

– maybe some other bands would take a bit from here, a piece from there. Then for a long time it seemed like I must be falling apart, although that didn't bother me because inside I felt good about what I was doing. And finally people started going, 'Hey look at that over there, that's a classic. And it's in pretty good shape.'"

Particularly good shape for one bent on auto-subversion. Though for some years the old clunker had been making some nasty noises (then, in the '80s it was a rare old-school artist who didn't), his ongoing scorched-earth approach to his own myth had been as defiant in its own way as Dylan's Newport folk festival electric set. Icons don't generally go in for long-term iconoclasm; it's too messy, tiring, upsets the businessmen. If Young's politics had become worryingly conservative, his music certainly hadn't, and while most of his peers still breathing had puffed along the same old path of perpetual fake-adolescence, he was still following his *Decade* edict and re-routing through the ditches either side.

If some of his old fans were less than appreciative of his efforts – "The Neil Young of the '80s," wrote Rolling Stone, "opted to become his generation's consummate weirdo, trivialising his monolithic accomplishments" – there were plenty of new, younger ones queuing up to take their place. Just as the punks at the end of the '70s had spared him from their death-to-hippies policy, and the post-punks at the end of the '80s had eulogised him on their tribute album *The Bridge* (which featured the likes of Sonic Youth, the Pixies, Dinosaur Jr, Nick Cave, Victoria Williams and Flaming Lips), in the '90s he would be hailed as Lord Of The Flannel Shirt by the disaffected, self-analytical "Generation X" twentysomethings whose music of choice was grunge.

Grunge bands not only sounded a lot like Neil Young, they looked a lot like him too with their lank hair, slackers' slump, anti-designer jeans and just-washed-the-truck checkered shirts. His ambiguity and confusion, jagged emotion and the contrast of his fragile keening voice and brutal, corrosive guitar, sat very comfortably with the mix of feedback and melody, cynicism and intro-spection favoured by the alternative rock movement that was emerging from the underground out into the charts.

"There's nothing different in what they're doing right now than what we were doing in the '60s; even the audiences look and feel the same," said the Godfather of Grunge as he summoned Crazy Horse to his ranch to make his first album of the '90s. *Ragged Glory* featured the kind of serious guitar work-outs absent from his albums for years. A raw electric record, sweaty, loud (when an earthquake struck nearby San Francisco on the last day of recording, legend has it no-one noticed) – it was like the '80s had never happened and Young and the Horse had just kept right on going after 1979's *Rust Never Sleeps*. A couple of its songs, in fact, had been written (and in typical Youngian fashion unreleased) back in the mid-'70s *On The Beach/Zuma* period, while the cover of garage-rocker Farmer John went back further still to his Squires days. Tracks like Mansion On The Hill, Love To Burn, Love And Only Love and anthem Fuckin' Up were greeted as a return to classic form. A fine way to start the new decade.

Its commercial and critical success prompted Young to forget his vow after the troubled Rusted-Out Garage outing never to tour with Crazy Horse again and, after an impromptu 45th birthday gig with them on the verandah of Mountain House, his local log-cabin restaurant on Skyline Boulevard, the four ravaged gunslingers took off for Prince's studio in Minneapolis to prepare for the tour. Young had raised the stakes by inviting some of his biggest young supporters to open up for them – Social Distortion and Sonic Youth. The West Coast hardcore band and East Coast no-wavers were not going to be easy to out-gun.

"Some of my audience thought I was crazy," said Young. "They had no idea what Sonic Youth was all about. And some of them thought it was kind of cool. I don't really care." He was too busy having a good time. Apart from damaging his ears with the volume, he was getting off on the sheer force and volume of his muscular playing. "Your physical condition has a lot to do with how you play," he said. "I'm tougher. I weigh about 35lbs more than I used to, and that's not flab." In fact, thanks to rigorous regular work-outs with the personal trainer he'd lent David Crosby to help work off his prison fat, Young was stronger and healthier than he'd ever been. He worked out on the road, too – his pre-show ritual was to sit in the space under the stage and do his stretch exercises while a somewhat consternated Sonic Youth played over his head. Crazy Horse had been banned from watching the opening act. "He felt it hyped them up too much and sped up the tempo during their own set," explained the Sonics' guitar/drum tech Keith Nealey.

Young's guitar playing during these 53 dates was incendiary as he machine-gunned the audience with his one-note solos and napalmed them with feedback. "It's not a macho display, like some bands have this strutting thing where they get up there and move around and they sweat and they pose," he said, distancing his approach from the guitar histrionics of the '80s stadium metal bands. "The sweating we do is because we're so far into it that we've forgotten how not to sweat. I start hyperventilating, my nose gets really cold and I feel this cool breeze blowing in my face when it's about 110 on-stage. You just get to that point where nothing else is there, it's just all gone and you're taking off." The brutal, apocalyptic jams and slaughterhouse howl were the perfect soundtrack to war.

As it happened, while the band were rehearsing, America and the Allies declared war on Iraq. Young immediately altered his set: "When something like that is happening, certain songs just seem trite. Why bother doing them?" He added a solo electric guitar version of Dylan's anti-war song Blowin' In The Wind – with typical confusion the man who favoured a strong US military and tied yellow ribbons around his mic-stand in support of the boys out fighting Operation Desert Storm had chosen a peace-flag for a backdrop. Backstage and on the bus he'd become addicted to the 24-hour CNN Gulf War coverage; on-stage he could picture bombs falling, buildings collapsing, dead bodies pulled from the rubble in his head. With his guitar playing he was trying "to recreate the sound of destruction, of violence and conflict, heavy machinery". It was captured on the 1991 live double album *Weld* – like *Live Rust* from a dozen years earlier, only louder. Here the frenzy of feedback was an essential part of the sound.

For those who hadn't had enough feedback there was more of it on optional-extra *Arc* – Sonic Youth guitarist Thurston Moore encouraged him to release the 35-minute album inspired by his band's closing number. "Because they were almost universally hated by the audience every night," said Nealy, "they would get their revenge by assaulting the audience with a 15-minute feed-back orgy, Expressway To Your Skull. Neil stormed in to the dressing room and gushed, "What's that last song you guys play? It's like Phil fucking Spector's Wall of Sound up there!" Young described *Arc* as "Elevator music for maniacs ... If you don't like rock'n'roll or speed metal then *Arc* is probably the most abrasive thing you could ever hear. It's made for people who want to hear it, who can envision themselves skiing downhill in their headphones, some kind of experience of velocity. There's no rhythm in *Arc*. It's completely free."

It was something that the British once again took more kindly to than his American fans. *Arc/Weld* made the UK Top 20 while not even approaching the Top 100 back home. The Number 1 album in the US at the time, incidentally, was by Seattle grunge band, Nirvana. The band that Sonic Youth had lobbied hard but unsuccess-fully to stand in for Social Distortion at their LA shows with Young was raising the fortunes of the label that had signed them after their indie debut: Geffen.

17 Unplugged

WITH *ARC/WELD*, THE CRESCENDO THAT HAD
been building up since *Eldorado* had come to an almighty
climax. And, after a climax, the options open to a man of
a certain age can generally be reduced to two: unplug or
have a rest. "The physical thing with the feedback, you
know, is it takes its toll on you," said Young on a VH1
documentary. "You either stop or you change completely,
because you can't continue it. I got to do something, I
want to play music, but I actually couldn't do any more of
that. I'd burned out on it. What you want is to get away to
the quiet, to things that are so small and quiet but when
you get in on them they're huge. It's like something under

a magnifying glass instead of something so big that it blows the walls off. I've gone to that extreme now."

He had to. The hearing problems that had caused him to cancel a couple of shows had been diagnosed as hyperacusis: super-sensitive hearing. Even a whisper sounded like Concorde taking off; there was nowhere to go but *quiet*. His 1992 shows were solo acoustic sit-down affairs with regular breaks to go back home to the wife and kids; his next album would follow a similar pattern but with the addition of a band. Writing a half-dozen songs, he made a list of the musicians he wanted to play them; it turned out they were the same ones who had played on *Harvest*.

Following a year of paying tribute to other people – the November '91 concert for promoter Bill Graham, who had died in a helicopter crash; the January '92 induction of Hendrix into the Rock and Roll Hall of Fame; his October appearance at the "Bobfest", Dylan's 30th anniversary celebration show – on the 20th anniversary of his enduringly popular *Harvest*, in November '92, Young released a tribute to himself: *Harvest Moon*. He'd been thinking about doing this "for years", he said; it was simply a matter of having the right songs. Plus once again he had a physical ailment that made playing his electric guitar too painful. His only caveat, when The Stray Gators and back-up singers Linda Ronstadt, Neil's half-sister Astrid and his former girlfriend Nicolette Larson joined him in the studio, was "at all costs to avoid making the same record over again. I think we succeeded."

The warm, resonant *Harvest Moon* was more contented and grown-up than *Harvest*. Quieter, too – "the quietest record I've ever made" – the peace after the war that was *Arc/Weld*. There was a good deal of gentle nostalgia – One Of These Days recalled old friends, Old King his dead dog, From Hank To Hendrix (the former applying equally to Williams and B. Marvin) his old heroes. It was an album about hanging on tight in the face of destruction, "trying to make things last, about survival and longevity, keeping relationships alive". It was, he said, "a more female record than any I've done", and he dedicated it to Pegi, "the woman of my life. Womanhood in general I think has had a big effect on my life."

Women, he told NME, "are very effective". At looking after him, certainly – from his mother Rassy funding, cheerleading and managing The Squires and ex-girlfriend Robin Lane fixing him up with Crazy Horse, to partners Susan Acevedo, Carrie Snodgress and Pegi Young protecting him from some of the rock lifestyle's more dangerous side-effects, giving him the security and solid base he always said he needed to come back to before he could take off again. "It's the starting point for my excursions into the outside world. If I didn't have somewhere I could call home, I'd be lost. I need it more than ever now, the older I get."

In the past Young seemed to have no trouble burning bridges, dropping women, friends and bands along the way in pursuit of his music and career. "I had to shit on a lot of people and leave a lot of friends behind to get where I am now, especially in the beginning," he told John Einarson. "I had almost no conscience for what I had to do. There was no way that I could put up with things that were going to stand in my way. I was so driven to make it." But now that he had made it, and for a while had seemed to be doing his damnedest to un-make it, things had changed. Having said back in '75, after breaking up with Snodgress, "music lasts a lot longer than relationships do", Young now declared, "The real music of my life is my family."

As 1993 rolled around, bumping carelessly over the January release of a compilation of '80s material, *Lucky Thirteen* (aptly subtitled "excursions into alien territory"; it failed to make a dent on the US charts) it brought with it a mellow, reflective, intimate Young playing songs stripped down to their bare acoustic essentials. A handful of US TV appearances captured the mood – six low-key concerts for the VH1 series Center Stage; songs from *Harvest Moon* played on The Tonight Show (the same programme he'd quit Buffalo Springfield rather than appear on) and Saturday Night Live; and, most famously, a performance for MTV Unplugged.

In the five years since the channel had banned Young's anti-rock-sponsorship This Note's For You, he'd long since been rehabilitated as revered elder statesman of the alternative rockers who paid the bulk of MTV's wages. But getting him to do an Unplugged was a complicated dance that involved initial distaste, then agreement, then last-minute cancellations, and the recording and aborting of an entire concert in New York. In the end, though, the chance to reinvent his old material for a new audience once again was too much to resist. Hunched over his acoustic guitar in MTV's Los Angeles studio, bushy grey eyebrows poking over a pair of opaque black shades, the stubborn, individualistic seeker of musical truth and beauty was captured on camera for a marketable slot on a medium that turned songs into commercials and provided an instant music fix for the spoon-fed video generation; he would have appreciated the irony.

The album *Neil Young Unplugged* (once more dedicated to Pegi) made a nice acoustic sampler for his new audience, and was for his older fans a fine acoustic companion-piece to *Weld*. Transformer Man, minus the vocoder and plus an auto-harp, was transformed, as was Like A Hurricane, the pump-organ giving it a sombre, affecting, churchy quality, and Young's cracked, soprano, more controlled than vulnerable, was on top form. "Few artists can get as much drama from so little apparent effort and nobody can cherry-pick material from his own archive so cleverly or perform it so convincingly," wrote Q. "The format could have been made for Young."

As the album, released in June '93, climbed into the UK Top 5, Young headed over with his band to play. Not *Unplugged*'s Stray Gators, but R&B band Booker T. And The MG's. They had met at Bob Dylan's anniversary show, where they'd acted as house backing band for the Bobfest line-up, which included Lou Reed, Stevie Wonder, Johnny Cash, Willie Nelson, Tom Petty, Pearl Jam and Sinead O'Connor (who had been booed off-stage in tears. Young, who went on after her, was unsympathetic: "There's nothing more creative than a volatile situation. If you're an artist preoccupied with what people think, you may as well give up"). Steve Cropper and "Duck" Dunn were in Australia touring with The Blues Brothers when they got the call from Booker T. that Young required their services for a European festival tour.

"Neil was having so much fun with this band," said Steve Cropper. "He even admitted to us – with all due respect to everyone he's worked with – that it was the tightest band he'd ever played with. He said to me, 'I never really have been able to relax on-stage, I've always been worried about this guy or that guy, but with you guys I don't worry about anything, I just go out and play.' He got so excited at rehearsal that he would sit down on the couch in his barn and pull out boxes of his sheet music and he'd be going through them trying to figure out another song we could do with him. I never really played Neil Young music before, I'm an R&B guy. I had forgotten how many great songs he had written. He knew all the lyrics to these songs and he'd just jump in and start playing them, and every time he'd do that Duck and I would look at each other and our eyes would get this big and we'd go, 'Not another one to learn!' The Finsbury Park gig was pretty awesome, I'd have to say, and there was a good one in Scotland, where Van Morrison played. Belgium was good and there was a big outdoor festival in Germany with Nirvana on the bill."

Anyone anticipating a Stax upgrade on The Bluenotes was quickly set to rights by the opening screech of feedback. His hearing problems forgotten, once again Young had recruited loud young bands for the US leg of the tour, including The Stone Temple Pilots and Pearl Jam. He'd tried for grunge's *crème de la crème* Nirvana, but they were too busy, currently back at the top of the charts with their second Geffen album, *In Utero*. It would be the last studio record the band would make. In May '94 frontman Kurt Cobain took his own drastic approach to iconoclasm: mainlining a milligram and a half of heroin, the 27-year-old, who had been turned on to Young by his favourite bands the Pixies and Sonic Youth, put a 20-gauge shotgun in his mouth and blew his brains out. His suicide note quoted from *Rust Never Sleeps'* My My, Hey Hey: "It's better to burn out than to fade away . . ."

18 Plugged Again

THERE WERE RUMOURS THAT YOUNG HAD been trying to contact Cobain shortly before his suicide – whether coincidence or because he sensed something was coming down will remain a mystery as long as Young refuses to talk about it. Then, it can't be easy knowing that, apart from a bullet, the last thing to go through a young man's dying mind was a song you wrote about staying alive. Young's thoughts on the subject appeared in the title track of the album he released four months later. *Sleeps With Angels*, recorded with Crazy Horse, was his lament for the musician he described as "one of the absolute best of all time".

The rock press rated *Sleeps With Angels* as one of Young's absolute best too, talking of it in the same breath as another album informed by death, *Tonight's The Night*. It had "the same unhinged, peculiar balance of sounds and the same rather desperate atmosphere", said Chris Heath's MOJO review. "Two years ago Neil Young told me, his tongue not quite in his cheek, that he will be going to heaven. 'I'm gonna go the low road to heaven. Down and through and then up.' His new album is mostly about the down and a little bit about the through. *Harvest Moon* was the best record yet made by a middle-aged rock star about getting your life together; the core of *Sleeps With Angels* is almost certainly the best yet about dealing with the debris when life falls apart."

Somebody else's life, that is. Young's was doing fine. *Sleeps With Angels* made the Top 10 on both sides of the Atlantic (hitting the Number 2 spot in the UK); his theme song for the movie Philadelphia had been nominated for an Oscar; he had received the Bammie (Bay Area Music Magazine) Award for Artist of the Year. He had jammed in a matter of months with Bob Dylan, Bruce Springsteen, Keith Richard, Johnny Cash, Jimmy Page, Simon &

Garfunkel, The Edge and half of Van Halen. He was about to re-sign a nice new record deal with Warners (set up by label chief Danny Goldberg, ironically Nirvana's former manager). And in January 1995 he would be inducted into the Rock and Roll Hall of Fame.

The man with the job of inducting him was Eddie Vedder of Pearl Jam – of whom Cobain's widow Courtney Love had said it was a shame that he wasn't the one who had shot himself. Pearl Jam had long been vocal Neil Young fans – they'd been covering Rockin' In The Free World in their live set for some time, and even performed it in their MTV Unplugged concert. Young's music, said Vedder after presenting him with the award, had been a big inspiration, which "taught us a lot about dignity, commitment and playing for the moment". Young's acceptance speech, perhaps less than diplomatic under the circumstances, credited Kurt Cobain as the inspiration for renewing *his* commitments. But his fondness for the band Kurt and Courtney dismissed as "grunge lite" was genuine. He liked their "soul and their big beat". Inviting them back to his Bridge School benefit concert (the same month, incidentally, that David Crosby was undergoing a liver transplant), he chose the occasion to perform My My, Hey Hey – a song that he said after Cobain's suicide he would never perform live again. By playing it straight after Sleeps With Angels, and with Pearl Jam in the wings, he was reclaiming the song as something positive. "You can only be cynical for so long, then after you've got that out, OK, great, what's next?" said Young. "That's where Pearl Jam is going, and it's good."

Two days after jamming on Fuckin' Up at the Hall of Fame ceremony, Young joined Pearl Jam once again at a Voters For Choice (pro-abortion group) concert in Washington DC. He had written a new song for the occasion, Act Of Love. Ten days later he was in the studio with Pearl Jam recording it. The song quickly turned into an entire Neil Young album: *Mirrorball* (and a one-off Pearl Jam single, Merkinball). Explained Young, "I don't like to go in the studio and work on just one song. Some people work for months on one song but I think I'd go nuts."

Bad Animals – the Seattle studio owned by stadium-rock locals Heart – was set up like a live stage show with Pearl Jam's longtime producer Brendan O'Brien at the controls. On the first day Young came in with three new songs; at the end of the session he booked another day, went home and wrote a few more – continuing the process for the four days it took for the album to be made. "Every 20 minutes Neil would say, 'OK, I've got something', and then he'd pull it up and we'd play it through once or twice and then we'd lay it down," said Pearl Jam guitarist Stone Gossard. "He'd just say, 'Here it is, G, C, D, G, C,D and the bridge is in B', and we'd all just hack along. It's definitely loose, but that's the good thing about Neil. He's not too worried about that sort of stuff and he makes it all right for everyone else not to worry about it."

"I think he's a genius," said the band's other guitarist Mike McCready. "There's a complexity to his playing, a complexity of emotions. He always hits the right note – I don't think it's a thinking process for him, he just does it." He was open, they said, to any suggestion or arrangement.

"If things are planned out too much and everybody knows what's going on and what's going to happen, there's almost no reason to do it then, is there?" said Young, who would play through a new song on his guitar, show them the changes, run through it with them a couple of times and then record. Speed was of the essence since Pearl Jam were due out on tour, and Young did not want to wait until they got back and risk losing the opportunity (as he had in the '80s with R.E.M. when a projected collaboration failed to come about), the desire or the vibe. It gave the album a raw, unrehearsed, knock-about feel that was part rusted-out-garage rock, part grunge. "Bigger, louder, older, stronger," declared the record company press release, getting it right for once. "They sing and play together like brothers," wrote Melody Maker, "not father and adopted sons." Pearl Jam "play like they're older than I am, with a lot of wisdom", beamed Young.

The combined buying power of Young's and Pearl Jam's audience made *Mirrorball* Top 5 in the US and the UK. Just months off his 50th birthday, looking like a particularly Neanderthal backwoodsman with his sprouting grey-brown hair, lowering eyebrows, thickset body and lumberjack shirt, Young found himself lauded in teenage heavy rock magazines like Kerrang!. "Most people my age don't do the things I do," sang the man they called Don Grungeone. Things like facing an angry crowd of 50,000

Pearl Jam fans at San Francisco's Golden Gate Park, where he substituted for Eddie Vedder on vocals when the singer quit the stage after seven songs with a stomach problem. Young enjoyed himself so much in the process he decided to give Pearl Jam Booker T. And The MG's' old job as his backing band on his European tour. "We hit it off," said Young. "They were a *band*, and that's exciting to get to play with a band. That's what was exciting about Crazy Horse and Booker T. And The MG's, that they'd played together for a long period of time."

The latest in his long list of line-ups went down as well with some of his older fans as his stint as Pearl Jam's singer had with their audience. Wrote MOJO's Barney Hoskyns of their Reading Festival appearance, "Seldom have I heard a band so devoid of feeling or so incapable of dynamics. Stolidly proficient musos to a man, they commence every song at full-throttle and build up from there. If Young thinks this is how you keep from fading away – if he thinks this is how you burn, let alone burn out – he is surely mistaken."

When a mirrorball turns in the light, a countless number of fractured images rush by. None of them stick around long enough to settle, but flash for a moment and move aside for the next one. The antithesis of *Harvest Moon*'s reflections about holding on to passing time, it made a fine metaphor for the channel-hopping, short-attention-span *fin de millennium*, and not a bad one either for Young's career.

19 Indians, Dead Men And
      Spooking The Horse

WHILE YOUNG WAS OFF TOURING WITH
Pearl Jam, Jim Jarmusch – the indie film director behind
Mystery Train and Stranger Than Paradise – was sitting in
a house in the Catskills, listening to Neil and Crazy Horse
albums on a boom-box and writing an existential western
called Dead Man. Young, it struck him, would write a
perfect soundtrack for his story of a 19th-century accoun-
tant named William Blake (played by Johnny Depp) and
his relationship with a literature-loving American Indian
named Nobody (Gary Farmer). Young thought so too and
improvised the music over three sessions while he

watched the film being screened, like the electric guitarist equivalent of a silent movie piano player. Released on his own Vapor Records in '96, *Music From And Inspired By The Motion Picture Dead Man* was a bleak, eerily hypnotic, solo instrumental work – imagine Cortez The Killer slowed right down, turned inside out and Arc-Welded, along with some storm sound effects, on to Jim Morrison's *American Prayer*. "Neil is very complicated," said Jarmusch. "Very contrary but in a good way, like some Native Americans. White men called them 'contraries' because they did apparently strange things like walk backwards or did things from the logic of a strange perspective. Neil has that perspective."

Later that same year Young returned the favour, inviting Jarmusch up to his ranch to make the video for Big Time, a track from his new album with Crazy Horse, *Broken Arrow*. (Its reviews ranged from "top stuff" – Q – to "the most dogged he's sounded in years" – MOJO.) Young liked the rough and ragged quality of Jarmusch's Super 8 footage so much that he asked him back to make an entire film.

Jarmusch: "Neil called up and said, 'Why don't you

come on tour and make a longer film that looks like Big Time. I said, 'How long a film do you want to make and what do you think we should do?' And Neil said, 'When I write a song I don't think about how long it should be; we'll just start shooting and see if we like it and if we don't we'll just throw it away. You decide what sort of film you want to make.'"

Although Young's fascination with moving images had far from dimmed and his camcorder still accompanied him everywhere, apart from a brief appearance as an ageing gangster in the 1990 movie Love At Large it had been 15 years since anything of his had made it on to the big screen. Muddy Track, the '80s concert documentary he had referred to as "my favourite; it's dark as hell but it's funky", still remained unreleased a decade later. Jarmusch would be working on its replacement, a documentary shot on Young and Crazy Horse's 1996 tour of Europe and the US, to be released with a live album – his third that decade counting *Unplugged* – with the same title, *Year Of The Horse*.

Jarmusch: "I already learned from working with Neil on Dead Man that he's almost shamanistic about his art. He has to have a circle drawn around him so that he has this place to go where nothing is going to interfere with him – all the bullshit business or social things – so that what he has inside could come out. He knows what process he needs to use and he's very demanding about having it – as he should be. He's done it for so long that he has to adjust his pace on the road – how many concerts they do, what kind of schedule they're on, how often they fly and what he does on the road. He likes to go to his room after a show and go on-line on his computer. They don't like to go out to parties all night – they've done all those things. They work out while they're on the road, exercise, they just stay pretty calm – a very different place to what it would have been 25 years ago. If they kept that up they wouldn't even be here anymore."

Along with some excerpts from Muddy Track, Jarmusch had incorporated footage from Young and the Horse's 1976 tour – the stoned, skinny, long-haired frontman barely recognisable in the stocky, muscular lumberjack wielding his chainsaw-guitar. Watching the rough cuts of the film with Jarmusch, Young jumped out of his seat at the scene where his '96 performance of Like

A Hurricane segued into the same song played 20 years earlier – he was shocked not at his own physical transformation but at the changes in his favourite guitar. "Wow, look at Old Black," he told Jarmusch. "She looks so different, so shiny and new. Maybe I should get her polished up. I haven't taken very good care of her."

Nor, for that matter, had he taken very good care of Crazy Horse, who just two years earlier had once again been unceremoniously dumped in favour of his latest fancy, a young grunge band. Not that they weren't used to it. "When I was younger I got pissed off," said Frank Sampedro, "but as I get older I recognise the fact that Neil always comes back to us and all these other bands he doesn't go back to. We are the one and only Neil Young band that survived all the cuts, so you get a certain sense of good feeling and security from that. And it's flattering to have him go play with some of those other people and know he'll come back and go, 'You guys want to play?' *Yeah*, we want to play!"

Billy Talbot: "We know each other so well now, we don't have to be together all the time. That spirit that we managed to create in the early years just carries on and on and on. It's like a family: you might not see your uncle for a few years but when you get together you have a lot to talk about and you're happy."

Like a variant on phantom limb syndrome, when Crazy Horse weren't around Young still would feel the itch. Poncho, Billy and Ralph gave him "a support that no-one else can give me, they afford me the possibilities of doing more with my guitar and my voice and feeling than anybody else . . . I know my musician friends, a lot of people, think we play simple, and the bass is so simple, there is no finesse and everything. But we're not trying to impress anybody, we just want to play with the feeling. We can play it very slow, we can play it extremely slow, but not fast. It's like a trance we get into."

Jarmusch: "It's something very transcending; when they pick up their instruments and play, they take off like some big bird flying into the sky. It's a magic thing – their lives and emotions and past histories having been linked for so long, they just shut their minds off and *feel* it. They remind me of John Coltrane's sheets of sound. One thing I think the film makes clear is the music comes from all four of them."

Ralph Molina: "Some people say it's Neil's sound, but when we got together as Neil Young and Crazy Horse Neil didn't have a sound. *We* didn't have a sound. He was with the Springfield, we were with The Rockets – I think that sound was created by the four of us." Said Sampedro, "It's the sound of one big guitar playing."

"And the older we get," added Young, "the more we realise how special it is."

Meanwhile, having cancelled at the eleventh hour their headlining appearance at Glastonbury 1997 (the invincible guitar player had been felled by the same thing that killed Mama Cass, a ham sandwich; he'd sliced the tip off a finger while cutting it up), Young got on with compiling an album to mark 10 years of concerts to raise money for the Bridge School, the place he had helped set up with Pegi to help disabled children like Ben. Thanks to the concerts, the school was equipped with the newest technology – something Young was very interested in himself.

In a joint venture with the owner of Lionel Trains – the popular American toy train company he'd bought and rescued from the sidings a few years earlier – he was working on developing a digital remote-control device that would allow two trains to run at different speeds on the same track. Young also had an electronics company which was experimenting with organic-based computers and new alternatives to compact discs. "Everything recorded between 1981 and, say, 2010 will be known as the dark ages of recorded sound," said Young, who had many reasons for disliking the CD. Apart from anything else, with the advent of the programming button, people could change and adapt an album to suit their own theme – anathema to a musician so concerned with controlling his art. There was also the small problem of him finding digital sound the equivalent of "sensory deprivation".

"It's almost like torture," he explained. "Digital makes you think that you're hearing it better than you heard it before [but] you're hearing a facsimile of it, you're only hearing the surface of it." With the coming in the '80s of the CD, he said, people had "stopped listening the way they used to listen" – that obsessive, head-between-the-speakers, repeated listening – because all they were listening to was "binary numbers being spat out of a digital converter that recreate the sound of music . . . You hear a CD once and you've heard it. You're not going to go deeper because there's nowhere to go." Although hardly a retro back-to-vinyl man. he was working on finding a new kind of durable but organic record you could love without loving to death.

Young, more than 30 years on, was continuing to fight his creative corner and in the process attracting an ever-growing and disparate band of supporters. No other veteran musician meant so many things to so many different people – gentle folkies, beer-swilling stadium jocks, stoned hippies, feedback-jonesing grunge kids, old married couples, loners and losers and the cream of independent-minded young artists. Beck – who appeared with him on *The Bridge School Concerts Volume 1* (alongside the likes of Tom Petty, Simon & Garfunkel, The Pretenders, Ministry and Pearl Jam) and at his other annual benefit, Farm Aid – spoke of the "importance" of Young's music when he presented him with an award for his charitable work.

"I remember the first time hearing a lot of these folk things of his and they were so simple, like some old shoes or an old hat that you just get addicted to wearing,"

Beck elaborated, "and that's one of the hardest things to do, to be that direct and unfiltered and simple without being absolutely trite. You can stick all the clever words you want together and come up with complex harmonic structures, but the song that can just communicate with you without any extra embellishments is very rare. He has made some of the most comfortable – and uncomfortable – music that I've ever found."

He was about to make a sharp U-turn back to the comfortable. Young's last album of the millennium would be a reunion with the group he first joined 30 years earlier, Crosby, Stills & Nash.

FORWARD BACKWARDS:
21ST CENTURY SCHIZOID MAN

20 Crawling Through The Desert

I don't mind dying, I don't mind getting old. But I don't want to be passive about it. I'm going to go fighting.

THERE WERE TWO KINDS OF RECORDS flooding the shops in the run-down to the millennium: tribute albums and retreads – motley musicians revisiting the best of a worthy veteran's back catalogue, and worthy veterans, alone or with the support of motley musicians, revisiting their own. Young, as was often the case, was ahead of his time: he'd had his tribute album way back in 1989 and by 1997 had already trawled through his own back pages five times – on 1977's *Decade*, '80s compilation *Lucky Thirteen* and on the three live records *Weld, Unplugged* and *Year Of The Horse*. Of his eight other '90s albums, seven saw Young still taking his dog-and-lamppost approach to music and musicians: darting from one, liking each of them equally, then rushing back to the one before for a sniff and perhaps another blast. "You've got to keep changing," he said. "It's like instant gratification. Then you go on to the next thing" – from ferocious feedback to the gentlest country, from solo acoustic to solo electric music; from Crazy Horse and The Stray Gators to Booker T. and Pearl Jam.

The eighth and last '90s album was perhaps the least expected. Where in the past Young had ended a decade on a musical high note – 1969's *Everybody Knows This Is Nowhere*, 1979's two *Rust* albums and 1989's *Freedom*, each featuring at least one member of Crazy Horse – October 1999's *Looking Forward* was a reunion with a group who had plodded pretty blandly through the previous decade and for whom his feelings had been ambiguous to say the least: Crosby, Stills and Nash.

The genesis of CSN&Y's third studio album in 30

years (and here the screen goes wavy and the words take on a sepia tone) stretches back to the post-ham sandwich period when Young, forced to cancel his tour with Crazy Horse, was hanging out back at the ranch. Dewey Martin and Bruce Palmer of The Buffalo Springfield were hanging out with him and playing – as much as Young could play with a bandage on his hand. Not long after, Stephen Stills came by too, helping sift through tapes for a Buffalo Springfield box set. Hearing the old material and remembering things past, Young was in uncharacteristically sentimental mode (though, one might say, not quite sentimental enough to play alongside Crosby, Stills, Nash and a host of veteran stars at the LA memorial concert for his former girlfriend Nicolette Larson, who died suddenly in December '97 of cerebral oedema). Stills picked up an acoustic guitar and played his old friend one of his new songs written for an upcoming CS&N album. Young offered to play guitar on it. Before leaving on a solo acoustic tour, he joined them in the studio in January '99 and stuck around long enough for it to become a CSN&Y album.

"Here's what it's like," said Crosby. "If you were

crawling through the desert and knew of a place where there once was a luscious fucking well, you'd go back to see if it was still there, wouldn't you?" Young, however, seemed to have little interest in deserts or wells. "I had some things to do," he said. "And I did 'em."

One specific thing he wanted to do was to make an album he felt realised the foursome's potential. As with The Buffalo Springfield before them, he was unhappy with each of the small number of records CSN&Y had made, thanks to a collision of bad recording techniques (ie not recorded live), outside distractions (ie drugs) and raging egos. He wanted, he told Stills, "to get back to where we started, before we became famous"; the fact that CS&N were without a record deal (their Atlantic contract expired in '96) and recording under their own steam was a bonus; it struck him as "pure". The next step was to wean them off their old approach of piecing together harmonies from separate takes and getting them to sing all together at one microphone, live (although he dropped the requirement when it came to adding vocal parts to three of the four already-recorded songs he brought to the party, Slowpoke, Out Of Control and the title track).

It might seem odd that someone who, in his own words, was "always like an add-on" – not only having joined after they were already a double-platinum outfit, but also being "the only person in Crosby, Stills, Nash & Young who was, you know, not Crosby, Stills and Nash" – should essentially be allowed to take over an album already in progress. The way Young looked at things was "I can be a team player, but I won't be a team player unless I can play my game", and the others had learned by now that a happy Neil was a co-operative Neil, and if he wasn't happy, "we better deal with it". If they didn't, their credible, successful suffix would walk. It wasn't always an easy job – "Satisfying Neil," said Crosby, "is something we've never been very good at in the past" – but Young declared himself quite satisfied with *Looking Forward*, feeling that it stood "right in there with *Déjà Vu* and *Crosby, Stills & Nash*".

The older rock press, glad to see them still kicking (not so much Nash, who'd broken both legs in a boating accident, but Crosby, who was sufficiently recovered from his liver transplant to father Melissa Etheridge's girlfriend's baby by artificial insemination), were kinder than they might have been. The buying public was less so, making it CSN&Y's poorest seller by a long shot (250,000 copies at the time of writing, compared with seven million *Déjà Vu*s and a million *American Dreams*). Young bullishly said they'd made the album they wanted to make. "I don't think we can ever live up to the myth that surrounded us in the first place," he told MOJO. "There's no way that any record we can make now would please everyone, so we just tried to please ourselves."

A tour was announced starting January 2000, some 40 sold-out arenas over three months. "We thoroughly intend to have as much fun as possible," Graham Nash said from his wheelchair at the press conference. They were setting up a special website so that fans could vote on what songs they wanted them to play. Young's idea, apparently. The artist who once upon a time had detested being treated like a human jukebox now chuckled warmly, "We won't have to do them, but we'll know what they want to hear." By all accounts, the least testy CSN&Y tour in history – aided by travelling in separate buses and staying at different hotels – the four were still taking it, like Alcoholics Anonymous veterans, one day at a time, even if the songs that sandwiched the set hinted at some kind of future: Carry On and Long May You Run. On the closing night in St Louis, as Nash announced this was the last show of the tour Stills corrected him, "No, it's the first show on our next one ... Welcome to CSN&Y 2001." Crosby kept quiet. As he'd said earlier, "You can't predict Neil. No-one except Neil can tell you what Neil's going to do next week."

The four Neil Young tracks on *Looking Forward* had been destined for his own record. Young had been working on a follow-up to *Broken Arrow* since '97. It was originally conceived as a solo acoustic album – completely solo, Neil playing all the instruments himself; he'd already recorded a handful of songs that way which he'd written while on the HORDE tour (the American summer event featuring local battle-of-the-band winners, whom the headliner was scouting in his role as Vapor Records boss). By the following year his plans had changed and Jim Keltner, Duck Dunn, Spooner Oldham, Oscar Butterworth and Ben Keith were brought back on board. The record's release was held up somewhat, Young having handed the tapes to Crosby Stills and Nash to pick whatever they wanted for

Looking Forward. Never that precious about his material – the prolific Young always seemed to figure that more songs would always come along – he took it as an opportunity to write some more, review what he had and dig around in the vaults to see if there was anything unreleased that fitted. He came up with Razor Love and Silver & Gold, which had been intended for the first, rejected, incarnation of his mid-'8os album *Old Ways*. Young had re-recorded the song 11 more times before it was right for the album to which it would give its name.

Warm, delicately-picked country guitar, rootsy harmonica, winsome pedal steel, Young's 21st-century debut brought to mind a *Comes A Time* Part II, though Warner Brothers – coffers open and fingers crossed – promoted it as *Harvest* Part III. *Silver And Gold* found Young not troubled, lost, haunted or curmudgeonly, not even particularly introspective, but *becalmed*. The album had one mood: comfortable, an untroubled feeling of effortlessness and ease – old friends kicking around on a back porch, shoes off, entertaining themselves and each other as the sun sank behind the trees on a mellow summer's evening.

"I had retired after producing Jewel's record and

bought a sailboat and moved to the Bahamas for two years," said Ben Keith, who co-produced *Silver And Gold* with Young, as he had *Comes A Time*, "and Neil called me up and said, 'I want you to come back to work.' He knew what he wanted – he always does: something very quiet and acoustic." His lyrics, like the easy-going music they recorded at the ranch, reflected Young's life as the new millennium rolled around every bit as much as *Neil Young* had expressed his state of mind in '69 or *On The Beach* in '74 – a mellowed 55-year-old contemplating where he was at and where he had been, washing everything with a golden sunset glow. The love songs spoke of the enduring contentment of a 22-years-married couple with grown-up kids. Roads and highways – sung about so often in the past – were now less places of unbounded freedom as obstacles that separated him from the comforts of home.

Released in April with an accompanying (live solo acoustic) DVD just as the CSN&Y tour was winding to a close, Young allowed himself a couple of months off the road before summoning the *Silver And Gold* team to his house in Hawaii to rehearse for his own tour. With his new-found talent for compromise, he had solved the problem of squaring his need to keep moving with his desire for settled domesticity: his wife would join his half-sister Astrid as a backing singer. "Pegi used to sing a lot before they even met," said Keith (silencing any murmurs of "Linda"); "they're just fabulous." As for Young, "He's become more mellow and more into the music than he used to be. It used to be a different thing with all the craziness that was going on back in them days; now it's more the music."

An eponymous live bootleg that surfaced from Virginia Beach soon after the Music In Head tour began backed up the steel player's assertion: a superbly played (the mellow numbers in particular), eclectic and often unexpected selection that started with Motorcycle Mama (*Comes A Time*) ended with Mellow My Mind (*Tonight's The Night*), and in between visited songs from *After The Gold Rush, Harvest, Rust Never Sleeps, American Stars'N'Bars, Harvest Moon, Decade, On The Beach* and, of course, *Silver And Gold*. An added bonus was Bad Fog Of Loneliness, a perfectly good song that Young first introduced 30 years earlier at the Cellar Door in 1970, and for reasons known only to himself had still not seen fit to release.

An official live album, recorded in a Colorado amphitheatre, was rushed out before the year's end: "Equal parts tantalising, frustrating and riveting," said Johnny Rogan's review of *Road Rock* in MOJO. Comparing it with the DVD from the same show that once again followed close in its wake, equal parts stimulating, disappointing and bewildering as well. Reducing the shows' 19-song set list (16 of which matched the bootleg's) to a rather puny eight for the album was always going to be difficult, but Young's choices sometimes seemed baffling – keeping Motorcycle Mama but shifting it from its opening slot; finding room for a not entirely essential duet with Chrissie Hynde on Dylan's All Along The Watchtower and still refusing to make an honest song of Bad Fog Of Loneliness, while granting legitimacy to the less worthy Fool For Your Love, a previously unreleased song from his '80s Bluenotes sessions. But with no indication of any UK shows on the itinerary, British fans were grateful for whatever crumbs they got.

Then suddenly, in Spring 2001, just as this book was going to press, Young announced that he would play a short UK tour after all. Not acoustic, but with Crazy Horse.

21 Boxing

ALL IN ALL, 21ST-CENTURY NEIL APPEARED
more motivated by love and acceptance than anger or
discontentment, more interested in building bridges
than burning them, and more than willing to be seen to
be looking back as well as forward. The CSN&Y reunion
had been remarkably trauma-free – no-one had walked
out, no punches had been thrown (then as Crosby said,
"we're too old to start boxing each other now"). And, if
the words of the *Silver And Gold* song Buffalo Springfield
Again were to be believed, Young was also tendering an
offer to his other former sparring partners to give it
another shot. Though he'd been saying much the same

thing off and on since he left them, nothing had so far come of it; he'd failed to show up for a reunion rehearsal in '86, 20 years after the band first formed (he'd "forgotten", he said), just as he was conspicuous by his absence at their induction into the Rock and Roll Hall of Fame. But he had been working closely with Stephen on the Springfield box set – said to stand at four CDs, at the time of writing it is still unreleased.

Also passing its Autumn 2000 scheduled release date was the first instalment of Neil's Big Project: a Beatles *Anthology*-type chronological history of his career. *Archives Volume 1* – said to comprise eight CDs and two DVDs (improving the sound quality of the latter was given as the cause of the latest delay) – was to cover the 1963–72 period and The Squires' early recordings, Buffalo Springfield rarities and Young's first solo demos made for Elektra in 1965, plus a number of early concerts in their entirety, including his 1968 performance at the Festival Hall and a 1970 concert with Danny Whitten and the Mark 1 Crazy Horse. Three more sets of CDs, adding up to 32 in all, had been "set up", he said, "so that when you put the whole set together it starts talking to you".

It was a "ridiculously huge" undertaking, the amount of material mind-boggling – not only thanks to Young's prodigious output but because he had assiduously recorded and videotaped almost everything he ever did. "I'm kind of like a freak for saving things," he said. "I have this urge to chronicle everything. I keep going, doing stuff for no reason, making films there's no buyer for. I finish them and put them away." He'd located around 98 per cent of this material (though by late 2000 the Mynah Birds sessions for Motown were still missing) and had been putting them in order – less a side-effect of his millennial outbreak of nostalgia than the pragmatic approach of a man who liked to be in control of his art and who wasn't getting any younger. "If I don't organise it," he said, "somebody else will after I die and it won't be right."

High-risk profession aside, Millennium Neil appeared less likely to keel over than at any point in his existence. "He's beefed up to 165 lbs and he's an axe murderer!"said Elliot Roberts. "People were always very afraid of Neil, but he was actually very frail. He's not anymore."

A sickly child, quiet and introverted, but with an

intensity that made everything, his music included, a matter of life or death, Young now had the physical strength to match his will. Truculent, stubborn, iconoclastic, he had always raged equally against the audience and the industry's attempts to box him in, as he had against any weaknesses, physical or musical, he perceived in himself. From listening to Jimi Hendrix albums with his roommates Jack Nitzsche and Denny Bruce in the '60s and analysing how they could have been better to constantly reevaluating, reworking and rejecting his own music, he was an anarchic individualist who craved structure and stability, an austere, moral, sometimes self-righteous man with an honesty bordering on arrogance, whom friends and associates would describe as a "prankster" and all-round barrel of laughs. A mass of contradictions – but it's what made him human and his music, if sometimes flawed, always emotionally compelling.

"I'm just like everybody else," he once said, "trying to figure out how it all goes together, or even if it does go together. Maybe it doesn't. Fine too."

Timeline

NOVEMBER 12, 1945 Born Neil Percival Kenneth Ragland Young in Toronto, Canada.

1961 Forms first band, The Jades.

1962 Forms The Squires.

APRIL 1965 Meets Stephen Stills at Canadian folk club, The 4th Dimension.

OCTOBER 1965 The Squires split up.

1966 Joins The Mynah Birds.

MARCH 1966 Co-founds The Buffalo Springfield.

1967 Two Buffalo Springfield albums released: *Buffalo Springfield* in January and *Buffalo Springfield Again* in December.

MAY 1968 The Buffalo Springfield break.

AUGUST 1968 *Last Time Around* – posthumous third Buffalo Springfield album.

DECEMBER 1968 Marries Susan Acevedo.

JANUARY 1969 Debut solo album, *Neil Young.*

MAY 1969 Album with Crazy Horse, *Everybody Knows This Is Nowhere.*

JULY 1969 Recruited by Crosby Stills and Nash.

AUGUST 1969 First gig with Crosby Stills Nash and Young at the Fillmore East.

DECEMBER 1969 CSN&Y play Altamont, RS.

MARCH 1970 CSN&Y album, *Déjà Vu.*

SEPTEMBER 1970 *After the Gold Rush*

FEBRUARY 1971 BBC TV and Festival Hall. Records with LSO.

APRIL 1971 Nash-compiled live CSN&Y album, *Four-Way Street.*

AUGUST 1971 Back operation.

AUTUMN 1971 Plays with CSN&Y.

MARCH 1972 Solo album, *Harvest.*

JUNE 1972 Records War Song with Graham Nash.

SEPTEMBER 1972 First son Zeke born.

NOVEMBER 1972 *Journey Through The Past* released. Crazy Horse guitarist Danny Whitten OD's, aged 29.

JANUARY 1973 US tour with Stray Gators.

APRIL 1973 *Journey Through The Past* film premiered at Dallas Film Festival.

AUGUST 1973 Records *Tonight's The Night.*

SEPTEMBER 1973 *Time Fades Away*

NOVEMBER 1973 UK tour with Eagles supporting.

JULY 1974 CSN&Y stadium tour begins.

JULY 1974 *On The Beach*

JUNE 1975 *Tonight's The Night*

OCTOBER 1975 Throat operation.

NOVEMBER 1975 *Zuma*

JULY 1976 Cancels a tour with Crazy Horse for a three-month
Stills-Young Band tour. Leaves tour after 18 dates.

SEPTEMBER 1976 Stills-Young Band, *Long May You Run*.

NOVEMBER 1976 Filmed appearance at the Band's farewell show,
The Last Waltz.

NOVEMBER 1977 Triple album retrospective, *Decade*.

AUGUST 2, 1978 Marries Pegi Morton.

SEPTEMBER 1978 Theatrical *Rust* tour with Crazy Horse.

OCTOBER 1978 *Comes A Time*

NOVEMBER 1978 Ben born – his second child, first with Pegi.

JUNE 1979 *Rust Never Sleeps*

NOVEMBER 1979 *Live Rust*

MARCH 1980 Pegi diagnosed with brain tumour.

OCTOBER 1980 *Hawkes & Doves*

OCTOBER 1981 *Re-ac-tor*

JANUARY 1982 Premiere, Human Highway film.

NOVEMBER 1982 First album for new label Geffen, *Trans*.

SEPTEMBER 1983 *Everybody's Rockin'*

NOVEMBER 1983 Geffen sues Young for making unrepresentative
records.

JUNE 1984 Tours with his new band, International Harvesters.

FEBRUARY 1985 Participates in Canada's Band Aid project,
Northern Lights for Africa.

JULY 1985 Appears at Live Aid in Philadelphia, both solo and with
CSN&Y.

AUGUST 1985 *Old Ways*

SEPTEMBER 1985 Appears at Farm Aid.

APRIL 1986 Plays at a Greenpeace benefit.

AUGUST 1986 *Landing On Water*

SEPTEMBER 1986 Rusted Out Garage tour with Crazy Horse.

OCTOBER 1986 Inaugurates and headlines star-studded Bridge
    School benefit concert. It will become an annual event.

JUNE 1987 Squires reunion in Winnipeg.

JULY 1987 *Life*

JANUARY 1988 Inducts Woody Guthrie into Rock and Roll Hall of
    Fame.

APRIL 1988 Re-signed to Reprise, releases *This Note's For You.*

NOVEMBER 1988 CSN&Y album, *American Dream.* Tours with new
    band, The Bluenotes.

JANUARY 1989 Records album, *Times Square* in New York then
    aborts it, retaining five songs for limited edition EP, *Eldorado.*

JUNE 1989 Solo acoustic tour.

SEPTEMBER 1989 Wins MTV video award for This Note's For You.

OCTOBER 1989 Releases *Freedom* and is subject of a tribute album,
    The Bridge: A Tribute To Neil Young.

APRIL 1990 Appears at Nelson Mandela tribute concert at
    London's Wembley Stadium.

SEPTEMBER 1990 *Ragged Glory*

JANUARY 1991 Tour with Crazy Horse. Sonic Youth and Social
    Distortion open. Several shows recorded for *Weld.*

OCTOBER 1991 *Arc/Weld* released.

1992 Inducts Jimi Hendrix into the Rock and Roll Hall of Fame.

OCTOBER 1992 Appears at Bob Dylan's 30th Anniversary
    Celebration concert.

JANUARY 1993 *Lucky Thirteen*

MAY 1993 Plays Willie Nelson's 60th birthday concert.

JUNE 1993 *Unplugged*, then tours with Booker T. & The MG's as backing band.

SEPTEMBER 1993 Appears with Pearl Jam at MTV Awards.

MARCH 1994 His song Philadelphia nominated for Oscar.

AUGUST 1994 *Sleeps With Angels*

JANUARY 1995 Inducted into the Rock and Roll Hall of Fame by Eddie Vedder of Pearl Jam.

JUNE 1995 Releases album collaboration with Pearl Jam, *Mirrorball*.

FEBRUARY 1996 Instrumental album from Jim Jarmusch film released, *Music From And Inspired By The Motion Picture Dead Man*.

JUNE 1996 *Broken Arrow*

1997 *Year Of The Horse* live album recorded with Crazy Horse.

FEBRUARY 1999 Starts solo acoustic tour, *An Evening With Neil Young*.

OCTOBER 1999 CSN&Y reunion album, *Looking Forward*.

JANUARY 2000 CSN&Y reunion tour.

APRIL 2000 *Silver & Gold* album and DVD released.

DECEMBER 2000 *Road Rock* live album released.

JULY 2001 Buffalo Springfield four-CD *Box Set* released.

Discography

The Loner/Sugar Mountain (December 1968)

The Loner/Everybody Knows This Is Nowhere (September 1969)

Down By The River/The Losing End (When You're On) (July 1969)

Down By The River/Cinnamon Girl (August 1970)

Oh Lonesome Me/I've Been Waiting For You (August 1970)

Oh Lonesome Me/Sugar Mountain (September 1970)

Only Love Can Break Your Heart/Birds (October 1970)

When You Dance I Can Really Love/Sugar Mountain (January 1971)

When You Dance I Can Really Love/After The Gold Rush (February 1971)

Heart Of Gold/Sugar Mountain (February 1972)

Old Man/The Needle And The Damage Done (April 1972)

War Song/The Needle And The Damage Done (June 1972)

Time Fades Away (live)/Last Trip To Tulsa (live) (October 1973)

Only Love Can break Your Heart/After the Gold Rush (March 1974)

Walk On/For The Turnstiles (July 1974)

Lookin' For A Love/Sugar Mountain (March 1976)

Drive Back/Stupid Girl (March 1976)

Don't Cry No Tears/Stupid Girl (May 1976)

Long May You Run/$^{12}\!/_8$ Blues (All the Same) (September 1976) with Stephen Stills

Midnight On the Bay/Black Coral (December 1976)

Hey Babe/Homegrown (July 1977)

Like A Hurricane/Hold Back The Tears (September 1977)

Sugar Mountain/The Needle And The Damage Done (January 1978)

Comes A Time/Motorcycle Mama (October 1978)

Four Strong Winds/Motorcycle Mama (November 1978)

Four Strong Winds/Human Highway (December 1978)

Hey, Hey, My, My (Into The Black)/My, My, Hey, Hey (Out Of The Blue) (August 1979)

Cinnamon Girl (live)/The Loner (live) (December 1979)

Hawks & Doves/Union Man (November 1980)

Stayin' Power/Captain Kennedy (February 1981)

Southern Pacific/Motor City (November 1981)

Opera Star/Surfer Joe And Moe The Sleaze (January 1982)

Little Thing Called Love/We R In Control (January 1983)

Sample And Hold/Mr Soul (January 1983)

Mr Soul/Mr Soul (part two) (February 1983)

Wonderin'/Payola Blues (September 1983)

Are There Any More Real Cowboys (July 1985) duet with Willie Nelson

Cry, Cry, Cry/Payola Blues (October 1983)

Get Back To The Country/Misfits (September 1985)

Old Ways/Once An Angel (November 1985)

Weight Of The World/Pressure (September 1986)

Mideast Vacation/Long Walk Home (June 1987)

Long Walk Home/Cryin' Eyes (July 1987)

Ten Men Workin'/I'm Goin' (April 1988)

This Note's For You (live)/This Note's For You (studio) (May 1988)

Rockin' In The Free World (live)/Rockin' In The Free World (studio) (April 1990)

Mansion On The Hill (edit)/Mansion On The Hill/Don't Spook The Horse (September 1990)

Harvest Moon/Winterlong (February 1993)

The Needle And The Damage Done (live)/You And Me (July 1993)

Long May You Run (live)/Sugar Mountain (live) (October 1993)

Rockin' In The Free World/ (remix) /Rockin' In The Free World (February 1994)

Philadelphia/Such A Woman (March 1994)

Piece Of Crap/Tonight's The Night (August 1994)

My Heart/Roll Another Number (For The Road) (October 1994)

Change Your Mind/Speakin' Out (November 1994)

Downtown/Big Green Country (August 1995)

Peace and Love/Safeway Cart (September 1995)

Big Time (edit)/Big Time/Interstate (July 1996)

ALBUMS

Neil Young (January 1969)

Everybody Knows This Is Nowhere (July 1969)

After The Gold Rush (September 1970)

Harvest (March 1972)

Journey Through The Past [soundtrack featuring live & rare material
  with past bands] (November 1972)

Time Fades Away (live) (September 1973)

On the Beach (July 1974)

Tonight's The Night (June 1975)

Zuma (November 1975)

Long May You Run (October 1976 as The Stills-Young Band)

American Stars'N'Bars (June 1977)

Decade [compilation] (November 1977)

Comes A Time (October 1978)

Rust Never Sleeps (June 1979)

Live Rust (live) (November 1979)

Hawks & Doves (October 1980)

RE-AC-TOR (October 1981)

Trans (November 1982)

Everybody's Rockin' (September 1983)

Old Ways (August 1985)

Landing On Water (August 1986)

The Best of Neil Young (February 1987)

Life (July 1987)

This Note's For You (May 1988)

Freedom (October 1989)

Ragged Glory (September 1990)

Arc/Weld (live) (October 1991)

Harvest Moon (October 1992)

Lucky Thirteen ['80s material] (January 1993)

Unplugged (June 1993)

Sleeps With Angels (August 1994)

Mirrorball (June 1995)

Music From & Inspired By The Motion Picture Dead Man (February 1996)

Broken Arrow (June 1996)

Year Of The Horse (live) (June 1997)

Silver & Gold (April 2000)

Road Rock Volume 1 (December 2000)